the smart approach to® kitchen DESIGN

Third Edition

CREATIVE
HOMEOWNER®

the smart approach to®
kitchen
DESIGN

Third Edition

Susan Maney Lovett

CREATIVE HOMEOWNER®, Upper Saddle River, New Jersey

A Division of Federal Marketing Corp.
Upper Saddle River, NJ

THE SMART APPROACH TO® KITCHEN DESIGN (3RD EDITION)

SENIOR EDITOR	Kathie Robitz
SENIOR DESIGNER	Glee Barre
PHOTO RESEARCHER	Robyn Poplasky
EDITORIAL ASSISTANT	Jennifer Calvert
INDEXER	Schroeder Indexing Services
COVER DESIGN	Glee Barre
FRONT COVER PHOTOGRAPHY	Anne Gummerson; architecture: Hammond-Wilson Architect
INSIDE FRONT COVER PHOTOGRAPHY	(top) Anne Gummerson; architecture: Brian Swanson; (bottom) Mark Lohman; design: Dana Jones, The Kitchen Consultant
BACK COVER PHOTOGRAPHY	(top) Eric Roth; design: Dahlia Kitchen Design; (center) Minh + Wass; design: Lorcan O'Herlihy; (bottom) Mark Lohman; design: Will McGraul & Co.
INSIDE BACK COVER PHOTOGRAPHY	(top) Anne Gummerson; architecture: Sara Schweizer; (bottom) Mark Lohman; design: Janet Lohman

CREATIVE HOMEOWNER

PRESIDENT	Brian Toolan
VP/EDITORIAL DIRECTOR	Timothy O. Bakke
PRODUCTION MANAGER	Kimberly H. Vivas
ART DIRECTOR	David Geer
MANAGING EDITOR	Fran J. Donegan

Current Printing (last digit)
10 9 8 7 6 5 4 3 2 1

The Smart Approach to® Kitchen Design (3rd Edition)
Library of Congress Control Number: 2006924701
ISBN10: 1-58011-317-6
ISBN-13: 978-1-58011-317-5

CREATIVE HOMEOWNER®
A Division of Federal Marketing Corp.
24 Park Way
Upper Saddle River, NJ 07458
www.creativehomeowner.com

dedication

I dedicate this book to my best friend, Juleen Peacock, who turned my kitchen into a work of art.

acknowledgments

I want to thank everyone who shared their ideas and experience for this book. I especially want to thank my family and friends for their encouragement and support. A special thanks goes to my editor, Kathie Robitz, who has touched me with her kindness and hard work.

contents

introduction

"The kitchen is now a microcosm of the whole house," observes notable architect Johnny Grey. "This is almost a full circle going back to medieval times when most families lived in one room." The new-again notion of the multipurpose room can create challenges for anyone planning a new kitchen. *The Smart Approach to® Kitchen Design* (Third Edition) can help meet those challenges by leading you through the process, one step at a time—from planning and financing to creating a layout, shopping for products and materials, choosing cabinets, and adding style. The information in this book, broken down into easy-to-understand "Smart Steps" and "Smart Tips," will show you how to make a kitchen work for the way you cook and live. Recognizing that many households are multigenerational, there's a chapter that addresses safety and special needs considerations for the young as well as older members of the family. *The Smart Approach to® Kitchen Design* (Third Edition) won't make you a better cook, but it can certainly make your time in the kitchen better spent and more enjoyable.

1

planning the project

THE RIGHT HELP BUDGETS LEGAL ISSUES LICENSES AND INSURANCE
HAVING IT YOUR WAY EVALUATING YOUR SKILLS DESIGN WORKBOOK
PERSONAL NEEDS DO IT YOURSELF?

While browsing through the photographs in this book, you will come across many ideas for your new kitchen. Visions of gastronomical feats or mere modest microwavable meals may dance in your head, but the road to an efficient plan will be full of important decisions about who will actually do the work and what it will cost. After all, the space you want to create may very well not only cater to you and your family's cooking and dining habits but also provide a place for you to pay the bills, the children to do their homework, or the entire family to indulge in hobbies. It's fine to window-shop, comb through books and magazines filled with appealing pictures, and make lists of all the things you want your new kitchen to be. Doing these things should be part of your homework, but you're going to have to take stock of the big picture.

Creating a kitchen that not only looks great but functions perfectly for the needs of your family requires careful planning.

The kitchen is truly the heart of the home. While committing to a remodeling project of this size can be intimidating and exciting at the same time, don't allow either your enthusiasm or concerns to cloud your way. To remain objective and keep from feeling overwhelmed, don't think about everything at once. Take it easy; slow down; and do your research. Once you have done all of this, then and only then are you ready to consider all of the options regarding who will be involved in all aspects of the work and how you will pay for it.

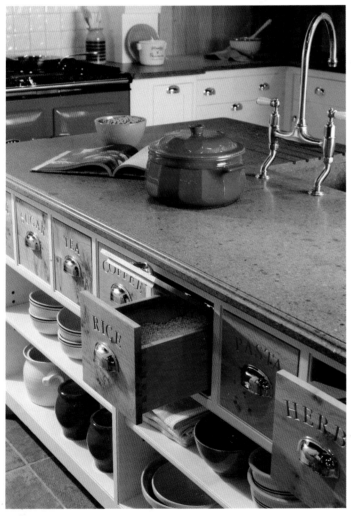

OPPOSITE
Plan to use durable surfaces and finishes that will stand the test of time. Choose a range, refrigerator, and microwave that suit your family's style of shopping, cooking, and eating.

ABOVE
Begin planning your new space by considering how you use your current kitchen. Think about the types of foods you buy and store. Count and measure the cookware and the serving pieces.

smart steps
a good place to start

Step 1 GET THE RIGHT HELP

Redesigning and remodeling a kitchen requires certain skills and knowledge. It is the most difficult and costly room in the house to remodel—not a project most do-it-yourselfers will feel comfortable tackling alone. In most cases, you will need to seek professional help at some point along the way, depending on your particular level of skill. But whom should you use? There are many different kinds of professionals who can assist you. Here is a short list of those who would be qualified to offer advice.

■ **Architects.** If you are planning a significant structural change in your kitchen, an architect is your best choice. Be sure to find one who specializes in residential design. However, the possible exception, if you are a very serious cook who often prepares meals for large groups, is a commercial architect who specializes in restaurant planning and would be willing to work on a small project. There are significant differences between residential and commercial design techniques. Although all architects are schooled to design both environments, someone who regularly designs kitchens for a family rather than an entire army or boardinghouse is better suited for your purpose. The letters AIA after an architect's name indicate membership in the American Institute of Architects, a national association with local and state chapters that readily offer referral services.

■ **Certified Kitchen Designers.** Called CKDs, these professionals are trained and certified specifically in kitchen design and remodeling by the National Kitchen and Bath Association (NKBA). Because they are specialists, they know the latest in kitchen products and trends and are highly qualified to devise the best layout and help you choose the most appropriate materials, fixtures, and appliances for your particular cooking and dining habits. Check local cabinet companies, kitchen and bath dealers, or a home center to find a qualified CKD. Or log on to the NKBA website at www.nkba.org.

■ **Interior Designers.** Interior designers can help you create and integrate style in your kitchen and throughout your home. They do not make structural changes but work with color, pattern, texture, and furnishings to shape a design. He or she will collaborate with an architect or other remodeling professional to create an overall look for your kitchen's design. You may want to contact an interior designer if you are making significant cosmetic changes to your kitchen. The letters "ASID" after an interior designer's name indicate membership in the American Society of Interior Designers, a national organization. For members to use "ASID" after their names, they must pass the National Council for Interior Design Qualification exam. Local or state chapters of the ASID can provide member referrals. Some states require licensing.

■ **Design-Build Remodeling Firms.** These firms offer one-stop shopping for design services and construction provided by designers and remodelers who are on staff. If something goes wrong, you only have to make one call. There is no passing the buck here: one boss, one client.

■ **Remodeling Contractors.** Some contractors offer design help as part of their remodeling services, or they are in partnership with a design professional. Contractors are good choices if you have already hired an architect to design the kitchen or if you are not making substantial structural changes to the room. One good example of when to choose a remodeling contractor is when you are simply refacing cabinets or reconfiguring the existing space for better efficiency in your kitchen layout.

Whenever you hire people to work in your house, take the time to research them carefully. Your home is likely your largest single asset; don't take chances with it unnecessarily. Interview professionals; inspect their

smart tip REFERENCES

Ask professionals for as many references as possible, but get at least three. When you speak to former clients, don't limit your questions to, "Did John Smith and his company do a good job?" You should be more detailed. Here are a few of the top questions to ask, as recommended by the National Association of the Remodeling Industry (NARI):

■ Could you communicate well with the remodeler?
■ Were you satisfied with the remodeler's business practices?
■ Did the crew show up on time?
■ Were you comfortable with the tradespeople that the remodeler contracted?
■ Was the job completed on schedule? On budget?
■ Did the remodeler fulfill his or her contract?
■ Did the remodeler stay in touch with you throughout the project?
■ Would you use the remodeler again on another project without hesitation?

portfolios; ask them for references; and by all means, follow up by checking their references thoroughly. Ask tough questions, both of them and their former clients. It's also wise to call state agencies and trade associations to inquire about the credentials of anyone you engage for the project.

Remember that whomever you choose to remodel your kitchen will end up knowing you and your family better than your lawyer or doctor. That person will see you first thing in the morning and will probably still be there when you come home after a long workday. It's in your best interest to scrutinize all professionals as closely as you would prospective tenants.

In addition to obtaining professional help, you will want to get first-hand advice from friends who have already been through the kitchen-remodeling process. No one source will be able to answer every question or meet every need, but the best approach is education. Clip out photographs in magazines for visual ideas; col-

lect notes and ideas; and hit the Internet and home shows on TV for further inspiration and handy tips that may save you time or money.

Take all these bits of information, and put them in one place—a dream book, a looseleaf binder, a drawer, or even an idea box. This is the fun part of remodeling. It is the time for fantasizing and making wish lists of all those design elements you have coveted for years—until your feet hit the ground and you wake up to the reality of money.

Step 2 ESTABLISH A WORKING BUDGET

This is the not-so-fun part—finding and parting with money. No one likes to crunch numbers, but establishing a budget is the only way to determine the size and scope of your project. It is very disappointing to plan a state-of-the-art kitchen that could rival any well-known chef's only to find you can barely afford a new cooktop and fresh wallpaper. Don't shy away from big dreams,

OPPOSITE
Your choice of materials, such as the color and finish of cabinets and countertops, the type of lighting fixtures, and the fabrics used for upholstery and window treatments, will imbue your kitchen with personality and style for years to come.

RIGHT
Classical details, such as columns and moldings along with natural materials, such as the wooden ceiling and the stone floor, provide this kitchen with Old World charm. Nevertheless, the space is packed with up-to-date, modern conveniences, such as the appliances, which include a large gas range and a dishwasher.

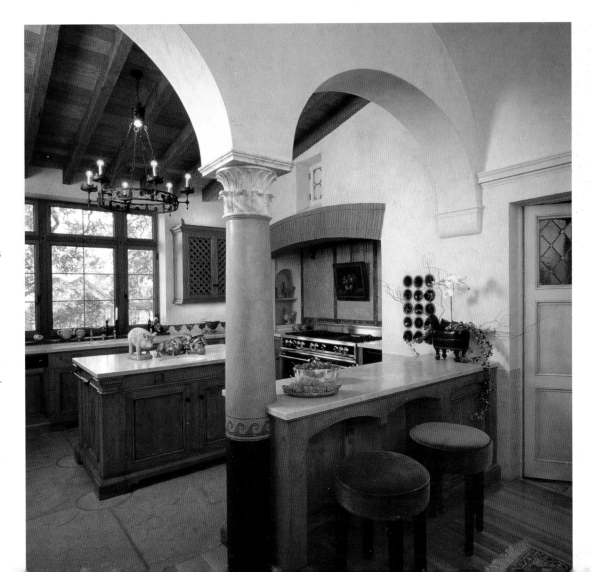

just determine what you can realistically afford to spend at this time.

Try to avoid paying cash for remodeling. If it comes down to a choice between paying cash for a new kitchen or for buying a car, it makes more sense to finance the remodeling. You can deduct the interest of the remodeling loan from your taxes; you can't deduct the interest on a car loan.

Step 3 LEGAL ISSUES

Anytime you enter into a formal agreement you are venturing into the legal world of a litigious society. As one of the contractual parties, you do have certain rights. For example, you can change your mind. This is called the "Right of Recision," which allows you to change your mind within three days of signing a contract without any liability if the contract was obtained some place other than the designer's or contractor's office—your home, for example. This grace period protects you against hasty decisions and hard sells. Federal law mandates making consumers aware of the right to cancel the contract without penalty. Ask your contractor about it.

You may also request waivers of lien, which release you from liabilities for subcontractors and manufacturers. At the end of the job, ask for a final lien waiver for each person who worked on the project so that you are protected from any third-party debts and obligations.

It's also a good idea to ask your contractor for a signed affidavit stating that all contractors have been compensated. You don't want to be legally forced to pay for a job twice because your general contractor didn't make good on his debts. With a lien waiver, you can refer an unpaid subcontractor to the general contractor for payment.

Furthermore, don't allow anything to happen on your property that is not in writing. If you want a change, get a written "change order." Remember, any change—whether initiated by you or a supplier or vendor—will cost more money. That's the nature of the game. Every change order should clearly describe what is to be done and how much it will cost. It should also include

RIGHT
A double-bowl stainless-steel sink and chrome gooseneck faucet with white ceramic handles work well in this cottage-style kitchen.

N

financing

Any bank or lending institution will be happy to tell you how much money you can afford to spend on your home-remodeling project. But if you feel more comfortable running a test on your own, here is a quick and simple overview of how banks figure out what you can spend.

The debt-to-income (DTI) ratio

This tells a lender if you can handle more debt on your current level of income. While each lender has its own approved DTI, the average is normally at least 45 percent.

Current monthly expenses	$_____
Add the estimated monthly remodeling payment	+_____
Total expenses	$_____
Divide by your gross monthly income	÷_____
This is your DTI	_____%

How to find your maximum payment for remodeling

If your DTI doesn't qualify for financing options, you may need to lower the monthly remodeling expenditure. This calculation will show you how low you need to go.

Gross monthly income	$_____
Multiply by lender's DTI ratio	x_____
Subtotal	$_____
Subtract your total monthly expenses (minus the estimated remodeling payment)	–_____
This gives you your maximum payment of	$_____

If the last line is negative, you may have to scale back your plans or do the work yourself on a very tight budget. A negative number means that you won't be receiving funds from a lender. However, you could check out other funding options. For example, a consolidation loan will allow you to incorporate your current debts into your home-improvement loan. Firstly, this will lower the monthly cost of your current debts. Secondly, this loan allows you to deduct the interest from your taxes, something that you can't do with other forms of debt.

Today's financial market offers a variety of other forms of financing as well. You could take out a loan against investments, borrow against your credit card, or the perennial favorite: obtain a private loan from family.

an estimate of how long it will take to complete the new work and its impact on the production schedule and project time line.

Step 4 LICENSES, INSURANCE, PERMITS

Ask to see the remodeler's license, if your local or state government requires one. However, just seeing it is not enough. It normally won't show expiration or suspension notices. Call the licensing agent to verify the status of the license.

All contractors should have current liability insurance and worker's compensation. The insurance protects employees of the remodeling firm while they are working on your property, so it pays to check it out before you allow possibly uninsured workers to place themselves in hazardous situations in and around your

contracts

You have the right to a specific and binding contract. The more details and pages it has, the better. Get specifics on every part of the project and on every product purchased. It is the details that will save you in the long run. Every contract should include basic items, such as:

- The contractor's name and proper company name, as listed on the business license
- The company's address and telephone and fax numbers
- The company's business license number if applicable (Some states don't require licensing. If this is the case, find out the company's business license and verify it.)
- Details of what the contractor will and will not do during the project, such as daily cleanup around the site, final cleanup, security measures to be taken during the demolition phase, and so on
- A detailed list of all materials and products to be used, including the size, color, model, and brand name of every specific product (If you have written specifications, you'll need two signatures to change them— yours and the contractor's.)

- The approximate start date and substantial completion dates during the project (You might ask for estimated completion dates for various stages; for example, one-third, halfway, and two-thirds through the process.)
- Your signature required on all plans before work begins (This prevents last-minute changes being made without your knowledge and prevents misunderstandings. This way, you get a chance to look at the plans one last time before walls come down and cabinets and sinks are placed on the wrong side of the room. One drawback to this provision is that it could cause delays if you are out of town during the renovation or are slow to respond. You may want to provide an address where you can be reached by overnight carrier or designate someone to sign in your absence.)
- Notification of your Right of Recision
- Procedures for handling changes in the scope of the work during the course of the project (The procedures should state how all of the change orders will be handled by the contractor. Change orders should require both your signature and the contractor's.)

- A listing and full description of warranties that cover materials and workmanship for the entire project (Warranties are normally in force for one year and should be identified as either "full" or "limited." A full warranty covers the full repair or replacement of faulty products, or your money is returned. A limited warranty indicates that replacements and refunds are limited in some regard. Limited warranty restrictions should be spelled out.)
- A binding arbitration clause in case of a disagreement (Arbitration enables both parties to resolve disputes quickly and effectively without litigation.)
- A provision for contractor's statements and waivers of liens to be provided to you prior to final payment

Include anything else that needs to be spelled out clearly. Remember: if it isn't in writing, it does not exist legally.

Most importantly, before signing any contract, be sure that you understand all of the components. You have the right to ask questions and to demand explanations. Never, ever sign an incomplete contract.

home. If you are still worried about your liability should an injury occur, talk to your insurance carrier and attorney. You may want to adjust your home-owner's coverage during the project.

Also, never allow the work on your home to be done without a legal permit. Permits may cost money and require inspections, but they can save you thousands in the future. In some states, if you have any work done without one and a problem occurs, you are held responsible. Years may go by, but when a tragedy such as a fire happens, you can bet that your insurance agency and the fire marshal will thoroughly investigate all of the possible causes. If faulty electrical work done during your kitchen remod-eling is to blame for it, the insur-ance company can refuse to pay the claim if there is no permit on record. This could be disastrous if the entire house burns down. Remember: nowhere in the home is the possibility of fire more likely than in the kitchen, where more building codes exist than for any other room. By obtaining a permit for your remodeling project, you are guaranteeing that a third party will inspect the work to make sure it complies with all the required safety regulations.

Step 5 HAVE IT YOUR WAY

It's your house and your money. Don't hesitate to ask as many questions as you like about any detail concerning the project. The more information you have, the happier you will be with the result. This is particularly true when selecting products or figur-ing out warranty coverage. Find out what is allowed under any warranties and what is forbidden. **Many manufacturers won't honor a**

warranty on an amateur "fix-it" job. To avoid disasters, call your contractor or the manufacturer for guidance.

Make your contractor sign for all deliveries during a job unless you personally ordered the materials or are prepared to be liable for them if the wrong thing is delivered or if something is damaged. Signing for materials is the contractor's responsibility. Imagine what would happen if you signed for an incomplete shipment or the wrong-size floor tiles. That's right, you're responsible for the mistake. Don't take chances.

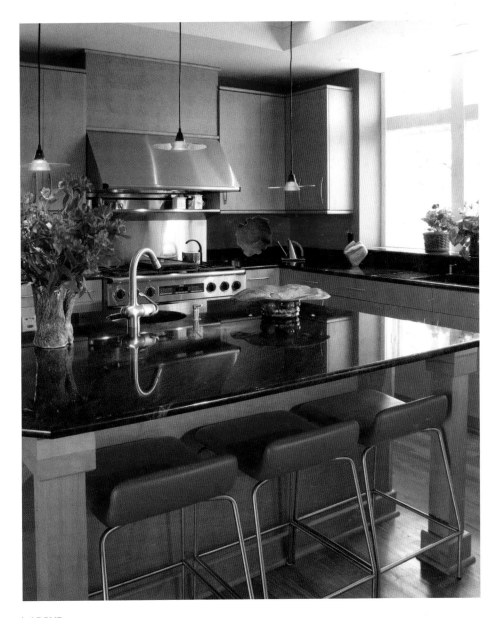

ABOVE
The stainless-steel range and hood, halogen light fixtures, and light-finish wood cabinetry with flat-panel doors provide a sleek contemporary look.

smart tip INVENTORY

The planning phase is the best time to clean out drawers and cabinets; count dishes, pots, and pans; and make a list of all of the new items you would like to have space for in your new kitchen. Don't forget about small appliances such as coffee machines and food processors.

Let your contractor shoulder the burden of tracking down incomplete or damaged orders.

Also, the people you hire to work on your house are in your home. You have every right to tell them not to smoke, play music, curse, or eat inside. You even have the right to tell them where to park and how to store their tools and materials around the place. Of course, you don't want to be unreasonable, but don't be completely put out either. Establish a set of rules before the work begins, and ask the general contractor to enforce them. Otherwise, do it yourself. Include your rules as part of the contract so you have a vantage point from which to operate.

Step 6 TALK THE TALK

There is nothing more frustrating than trying to communicate with someone who doesn't speak your language. That is how it can feel, sometimes, when you're trying to talk to someone outside your profession. We all have our own jargon and feel at a disadvantage if we can't use the language of the trade. If you are going to remodel, check out the glossary in the back of this book for commonly used terms in kitchen remodeling.

In addition, decide how you are going to convey problems to your contractor. Again, if you know how you will respond if something goes wrong, you won't panic. If you don't handle stress well, someone else in the household should take over the day-to-day communication with the contractor; maybe your talents could be better spent in the early planning stages and the final decoration.

Step 7 PREPARE YOURSELF EMOTIONALLY

Remodeling is stressful, even if you do the work yourself (perhaps especially if you do the work yourself). It's hard to deal with the sawdust and noise and constant inconvenience of not having a finished kitchen. At times it will seem like the project is something that is being done to you, rather than for you. But there are ways to ready yourself and your family for the temporary upheaval that could last weeks or even a few months.

Begin by talking to everyone in the family about

OPPOSITE
Stainless-steel appliances and countertops paired with a glass-tile backsplash not only modernize a space, but will prove easy to maintain over time.

ABOVE
If you cook lots of pastas or soups, a pot filler, such as this handsome unit, installed just above the range, will save you many steps with heavy pots.

permits

If your contractor asks you to apply for the permit yourself, refuse. Most jurisdictions consider the person who obtained the permit to be the general contractor and the one responsible for the outcome of the job. The county or building officials in your jurisdiction will come to you if the work is not up to code during the inspection. If these officials have a problem, it is far better to let them talk to a professional.

If you are doing the work yourself, be sure to find out the laws in your particular area. Some types of work require that a licensed professional meet code; many jurisdictions won't accept amateur work on electrical systems, for example, because the result of an error can be tragic. Keep the permit for future reference.

what is involved. If strangers will be in your home, let your family meet them before the project begins. Your house is your most personal asset and your most private retreat. It is essential that you and your family know how to protect it and yourselves before there are unfamiliar faces walking in and around the place. Also, plan ahead for times when the kitchen is completely off limits. Include a stipend in your budget for restaurant meals and take-out food.

Contractors often talk of what they call the "remodeling curve"—the wave of ups and downs everyone involved in remodeling goes through. Some days are good (such as when the framing is done) and some days are bad (when it looks as if nothing has happened in days). This is normal. What helps is to talk with your family about it, expect it, and prepare for it.

Decide ahead of time to get away for a few days when you feel as if nothing is going the way everybody would like, even if it's just for the weekend. You can stave off the frustration by anticipating it, and you'll feel more in control if you have a plan of action.

Step 8 EVALUATE YOUR SKILL

This analysis is a great idea if you are contemplating doing the renovation yourself. We have all seen the various do-it-yourself (DIY) cable shows that make everything look so easy. But don't forget that those shows are run by professionals who have the tools, experience, skills, and assistants that are necessary to do it successfully the first time. Can you remodel the kitchen on your own? That depends. Take the National Association of the Remodeling Industry (NARI) quiz on

OPPOSITE
Cabinetry with the look of fine furniture integrates this kitchen almost seamlessly into adjacent living spaces. Another idea: use the same flooring material to help visually unite adjoining spaces.

RIGHT
A section of raised countertop serves two functions, forming a snack bar and concealing any meal prep clutter.

the next page to get an idea of whether or not you should attempt the task yourself.

NARI says that if you marked a majority of the answers "yes," you may want to attempt doing the job yourself. But before you strap on a carpenter's belt, revisit those marked "no." Consider the problems you may face in those areas. Hiring a professional may still be your best option. Or you can compromise: hire a professional for the technical and difficult aspects of the job, such as the plumbing or the installation of the cabinets, and do the cosmetic work yourself. Only you can decide the best course of action for your skill level and project.

For additional advice about all of these issues, visit the NARI Web site (www.nari.org). You'll find a homeowner's guide that addresses the most frequently asked questions about remodeling, money tips, contracting matters, and more.

ABOVE LEFT
Refrigerators and freezers concealed in drawers are widely available and are convenient and easy for family members of all sizes and abilities to access.

LEFT
If your kitchen space is large enough to accommodate a table and chairs, look for an updated version of the classic kitchen dinette set to provide comfortable seating for four or more.

should you do it yourself?

Should you do it yourself? Remodeling a kitchen is a time-consuming and complex project. If you're thinking of handling the task on your own, take a few minutes to evaluate your skills and abilities by answering the following questions.

Yes	No	
Yes	No	Do you enjoy physical work?
Yes	No	Are you persistent and patient? Do you have reliable work habits? Once the project is started, will it get finished?
Yes	No	Do you have all the tools needed and, more importantly, the skills required to do the job?
Yes	No	What level of quality do you need for this project? Are your skills at that level?
Yes	No	Do you have time to complete the project? (Always double or triple the time estimated for a DIY project, unless you are highly skilled and familiar with that type of project.)
Yes	No	Will it matter if the project remains unfinished for a period of time?
Yes	No	Are you prepared to handle the kind of stress this project will create in your family relationships?
Yes	No	Have you done all of the steps involved in the project before?
Yes	No	Have you obtained the installation instructions from the manufacturers of the various products and fixtures to determine whether this is a project you still want to undertake? (You can obtain them from most manufacturers before purchase to determine the steps involved in installation and the skill level required.)
Yes	No	Is this a job you can accomplish completely by yourself, or will you need assistance? If you'll need help, what skill level is involved for your assistant? If you need a professional subcontractor, do you have access to a skilled labor pool?
Yes	No	Are you familiar with local building codes and permit requirements? (Check into these matters before beginning work on your kitchen project.)
Yes	No	What will you do if something goes wrong and you can't handle it? (Most contractors are wary about taking on a botched DIY job, and many just won't. The liability is too high.)
Yes	No	Is it safe for you to do this project? (If you are unfamiliar with roofing [for a kitchen addition] or do not have fall-protection restraints, you may not want to venture a roofing job. Similarly, if you know nothing about electricity, leave it to the professionals. Some jobs can have serious consequences if not performed correctly. Your health and safety should be the primary concerns.)
Yes	No	Can you obtain the materials you need? Who will be your supplier?
Yes	No	Are you attempting to do it yourself for financial reasons? If so, have you looked at all your costs, including the cost of materials, your time, and the tools you need to purchase? If you are new to the DIY game, you may also want to consider the cost to correct any mistakes you may make. Will it still be a cost-saving venture given all of these factors?
Yes	No	If you are trying DIY for your personal satisfaction, can you really guarantee a job that will be well done? If it doesn't come out right, how will you feel? Will you need the money to redo any unsatisfactory work? Will you have it? Will you be able to live with mistakes?

design workbook
DETAILS MAKE A DIFFERENCE

natural light

Abundant natural light coming in from large windows enhances the warm honey tones used in this kitchen.

the view

Consider what you'll be looking at outdoors when locating windows in your new kitchen. (See also top left.)

point-of-use faucets

If your kitchen will include two separate sinks, match the style and finish of the faucets. (See also far left.)

functional lighting

Include lighting fixtures that stylishly illuminate work areas and the room in general. (See also middle left.)

accent lighting

Showcase glassware and china with accent lighting that can be installed inside glass-door cabinets (left).

design workbook
TRADITION REIGNS

farmhouse chic

Elegant cabinetry and traditional details that include moldings, light sconces, and cabinet pulls, set the semiformal tone of this up-to-date and easy-care farmhouse-style kitchen.

cook's space

Provide the cook with plenty of countertop landing space on either side of the cooktop. (See also top left.)

furniture details

The kitchen island, with tavern-table-style legs, resembles a piece of furniture. Similar details include the cabinets' "unfitted" look and antique-white finish.

apt use of fabric

Fabric charmingly hides the drawer below the sink and items stored inside a cabinet with wire-mesh door inserts (left and far left).

Many factors, including the size of the space and the number of doorways and windows, will affect the layout of your kitchen.

choose a layout

GETTING STARTED   CONFIGURING SPACE   CREATING A LAYOUT
DESIGN WORKBOOK

You probably find yourself in the kitchen many times throughout the day doing much more than cooking. You may get together there with friends, pay the bills at the table, plan the family vacation, or design a craft project. All of that is in addition to the kitchen's traditional function as a place to prepare food. This one room has become so important, in fact, that prospective buyers consider it a primary factor in selecting a home. If you're thinking about remodeling the kitchen for resale purposes, you'll be happy to know you may get as much back as you invest—maybe more, depending on where you live. If you're like most people, however, your motivations for making changes are much more personal. The photographs and ideas presented in this chapter offer numerous ways to take the best advantage of any space, large or small.

getting started

Wouldn't it be delightful to prepare a meal in a kitchen equipped with the latest appliances and configured to let you move effortlessly from refrigerator to sink to cooktop without tripping over the kids, the cat, or your own feet? Imagine opening a cabinet without having to strain or empty the entire contents to find one small can. Picture a countertop that isn't a catchall for the mail, dry cleaning receipts, phone books, and all the rest of the cabinet and drawer spillover. Think about enjoying breakfast or eating dinner in a space that isn't in full view of the cooking mess.

Besides the basics of cooking and cleanup, today's kitchen designs often include room for special pursuits or hobbies. Gourmets grappling with the complexities of gastronomic fare may find professional-style equipment and dedicated work areas handy. The "office" may find a home in the kitchen, too, with space allocated for a desk, computer and printer, and possibly a small filing cabinet.

The place to start, then, is with how you want the kitchen to work—for you and every other member of your household. Function is the cornerstone of good kitchen design. A highly functional kitchen will not make you a master chef or change your attitudes about cooking, but it will improve the quality of the time you spend in the kitchen, which some experts report can be as much as 70 percent of your waking hours. With this in mind, remember: even the smallest remodeling job requires careful planning and forethought. You can greatly increase the efficiency and performance of your kitchen by paying attention to the tiniest details and the smallest of spaces.

Design professionals interview their clients at length at the beginning of a project. If you will be your own designer, do the same. Likewise, you may even want to videotape your family (and yourself) in the kitchen during typical meal preparation or any other kitchen-based activities. If your parties often spill into the kitchen, for instance, videotape the next gathering, and pay attention to how difficult or easy it is to interact with guests while you're cooking or serving. Is there enough room for opening the refrigerator door when someone passes behind you?

Is there space on the countertop to set up a small, informal buffet or bar so guests can help themselves while you're busy with last-minute tasks?

Note the different situations that typically interrupt or assist your work flow and traffic patterns. Is the aisle you use to reach the oven the same as the one used to walk from the back door into the house? Observe how many times you have to walk across the room for something.

LEFT
Cabinetry or appliances placed on an angle often make the best use of corners. Consider if your room is large enough to accommodate an island and the necessary passing space around it.

OPPOSITE
A massive fireplace is well-suited to a kitchen with high ceilings.

RIGHT
Curved walls and contemporary finishes complement an open floor plan.

OPPOSITE
If space permits, an island offers the opportunity to add storage, countertop workspace, and a breakfast bar, such as the one in this traditionally styled, family-friendly kitchen.

smart tip REFERENCES

Ask professionals for as many references as possible, but get at least three. When you speak to former clients, don't limit your questions to, "Did John Smith and his company do a good job?" You should be more detailed. Here are a few of the top questions to ask, as recommended by the National Association of the Remodeling Industry (NARI):

- Could you communicate well with the remodeler?
- Were you satisfied with the remodeler's business practices?
- Did the crew show up on time?
- Were you comfortable with the tradespeople that the remodeler contracted?
- Was the job completed on schedule? On budget?
- Did the remodeler fulfill his or her contract?
- Did the remodeler stay in touch throughout the project?

If you consult with a professional, don't be put off by questions. Any good designer has to get to know the habits, likes, and dislikes of the people who will live with the finished project. This person wants to understand your basic requirements in addition to your wildest dreams in order to meet most, if not all, of your expectations.

A designer will also sketch the existing space to get an idea of what works and what doesn't. This rough drawing may include any adjacent areas that might be considered for expansion, such as a pantry or part of a hallway. Once again, if you act as your own designer, do the same. Talk to everyone in the household. Ask what they think needs improvement, as well as any aspects of the space as it exists that they'd prefer to retain. Find out whether anyone has suggestions for solving any functional problems.

For the best results, approach your new kitchen project in the same calm analytical manner as a professional, one who understands design and can be objective about what has to happen and when.

smart steps
planning basics

■ ### Step 1 CREATE A DESIGN NOTEBOOK

It's important to keep all your ideas and records in one place. Buy a loose-leaf binder, and use it to organize everything from magazine clippings to photos of the old kitchen (extremely important if you choose to resell the house); wish lists; notes and interviews with design professionals and family members; contracts; sample plans; shopping lists; color charts; tile, fabric, and wallpaper samples; and anything else related to the project. The file should be comprehensive yet not too clumsy so that you can take it along when you visit kitchen showrooms or stores.

■ ### Step 2 ANALYZE THE EXISTING KITCHEN

Decide what you really want to gain by remodeling. You might begin by asking the most obvious question: what's wrong with the existing kitchen? Maybe you and your partner enjoy cooking together, but the floor plan was designed to work for only one cook. Perhaps storage is inadequate or the appliances are old. Or maybe it just looks dated.

To be specific about your analysis, get out your notebook and record answers to questions such as: is the size of the family likely to grow or shrink in the near future? If the kids are or will be away at college soon, you really might not need that large-capacity refrigerator. Likewise, if this is your first house and you expect to move up as your family size increases, it might be wise to simply refinish high-ticket items like cabinets and hang onto older appliances that are still in working order, spending only a modest amount of money, time, and energy on cosmetic changes.

Note how each family member uses the kitchen. How many really cook? What kind of meals? Full-course dinners? Microwavable snacks? Ask everyone, including yourself, to list five items in the current kitchen they couldn't live without, and another five items they would gladly give up.

How convenient is it to work in the kitchen? Are people always bumping into each other? When cabinet or appliance doors are open, is the traffic pattern interrupted? Are the sink and countertop at a comfortable height? Are faucet and appliance controls easy to reach and handle? You can change any of these situations to your liking.

How many people in the family use the kitchen at the same time? Separate task areas become even more important when two or more people work in the kitchen simultaneously. Who is the main cook? He or she should make the decision about the preferred cooking fuel. Will it be gas, electric, halogen, microwave, or a combination? Keep in mind that the answer will dictate the choice of appliances.

Other questions in your analysis might include: does

the family eat most meals together or separately? Do you need an eat-in kitchen with a built-in booth or a separate dining table, or will a snack island do?

If anyone in the family has physical limitations, implement changes that make the kitchen functional for everyone. Keep traffic aisles unobstructed or lower the countertops, for example.

Is the kitchen too small? Too dark? Can you add on? If not, look at adjacent areas. Is there a pantry, hallway, or part of another room you can incorporate into the kitchen? Would an additional window or skylight make the space feel more open? If you would like to make the kitchen accessible to outdoor living areas, are French doors an option? What other forms of entry are possible?

One common complaint about existing kitchens is the lack of storage. If space limitations have forced you to keep kitchen- or cooking-related items in other rooms of the house, it's time to analyze how to increase the storage capacity in the kitchen. If you go shopping once a month to stock up or shop in bulk, a roomy pantry—perhaps in addition to a large-capacity refrigerator and freezer—may help. Even if you can't increase the total linear feet of cabinetry in the kitchen, you can maximize what you have. On the other hand, if you eat out several nights a week, entertain rarely, or buy produce and meat or fish daily, you might find other uses that are of more importance to you for what would otherwise be storage space.

What else would you like to include in the kitchen if you had the room—laundry facilities, an ironing board, cleaning or craft supplies, pet food? If you have young children who need supervision while you prepare dinner, how about a place to house games, coloring books, crayons, and the like? Would you like to reserve a cabinet—out of your way—for snacks for the older kids and their friends?

Evaluate the condition of existing materials and appliances. How old are they? Are the appliances energy-efficient? Are the walls, floors, and countertops in good condition? If they are just outdated, you'll still probably want to replace or refinish them to add a fresh face to the new design.

There are other issues to think about, as well. You may prefer a design that's open to the family room or other public areas of the house. Others may want to close off the kitchen—and the mess of meal preparation—to everyone but the cook and cleanup crew. Then there are people who almost live in their kitchen. If you are among them, do your guests hang out there during meal preparation? Do you watch TV while mashing the potatoes? Do you pay the bills, paint crafts, or do other chores at the kitchen table? Do you need a comfortable chair next to the phone? Would you enjoy a small sofa or a fireplace in the room?

Planning includes being realistic about the future, too. This means anticipating an aging, expanded, or

OPPOSITE
Cooking area convenience features include durable, wipe-clean surfaces, such as a stainless-steel range and tile backsplash.

LEFT
This island serves several functions, separating the kitchen work areas from adjacent living spaces, housing the sink and cleanup area, and providing a space for cookbook storage.

BELOW
If you don't use the microwave at mealtime, locate it outside the main food-preparation area.

reduced-size household, or perhaps even moving. Weigh these factors with what needs improvement and any other details you don't want to overlook.

Step 3 MAKE A WISH LIST

Besides the basic elements, you may want some special features in your new kitchen—a ceramic glass-top range, modular refrigeration, interchangeable cooktop components, or a warming drawer. Perhaps an elegant granite countertop or a gorgeous custom-tiled range hood has caught your eye.

Create a list of all the accoutrements you would like to include, whether or not you think you can afford them. When you have a close-to-perfect plan, that's the time to look for areas to trim if your budget is tight. You might opt for a countertop fabricated in an affordable stone lookalike and use the dollars saved for something you can't fake, like an energy-efficient window over the sink, a pair of French doors, or a six-burner cooktop with a grill insert.

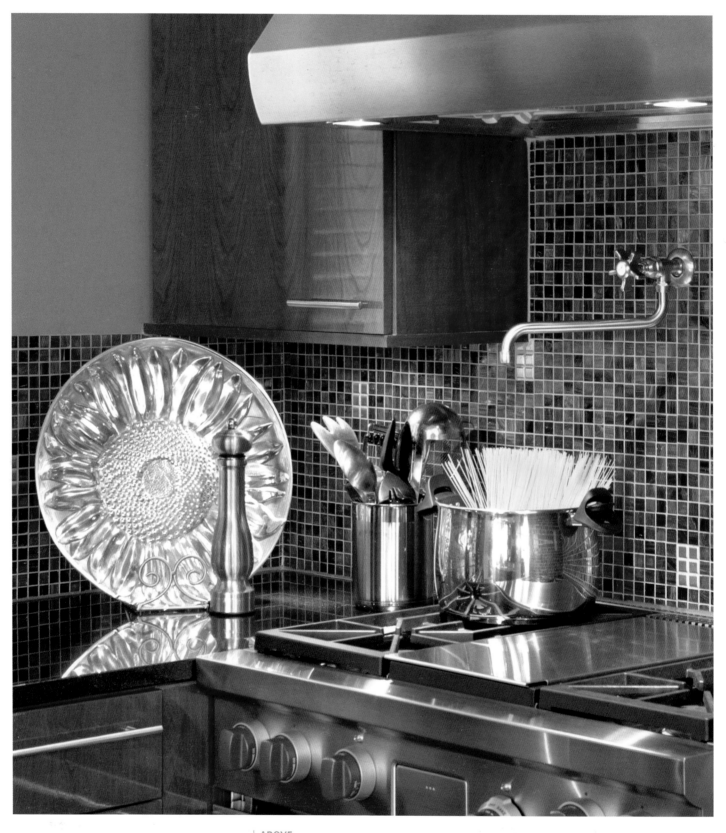

ABOVE
The serious cook will appreciate details like this pot filler and the heavy-duty grates that allow you to slide hefty pots rather than lift them from one burner to another.

ABOVE **Make a rough freehand drawing of your existing kitchen, recording accurate measurements as you take them.**

ABOVE **Transfer all of the information you've compiled onto a scaled drawing done on graph paper.**

You'll find lots of ideas for your new kitchen, including what types of materials to use and what appliances and features are right for your lifestyle and your budget, by reading this book, researching various items on the internet, and even by watching TV. As you compile your wish list, note everything that fulfills your fantasies, as well as practical items that need to be added or replaced. Be sure to visit showrooms and home centers, too. Talk to salespeople and professionals who can tell you about new product introductions, which seem to appear almost daily.

Step 4 SKETCH THE OLD FLOOR PLAN

Just like a professional designer, draw an existing floor plan. Do a rough sketch first, and then transfer your drawing to graph paper with grids marked at ¼-inch intervals. Draw the sketch freehand or with a straight-edge, but do it to a scale of ½ inch equal to one foot. This base plan, or "base map," as it is called, should record the layout of the space as it currently exists. Include measurements for everything, from the width of every doorway to how far the refrigerator protrudes into the room.

Start by taking measurements, beginning with the length and width of the room. Then from one corner, measure the location of windows, doors, and walls. Record the swing of each door. Write each dimension in feet and inches to the nearest ¼ inch.

Next draw the cabinetry and appliances, and indicate their height. Measure the position and centerline of the sink (showing how far the center of this fixture is from the wall), but don't forget to list its overall length and width. Also, measure the height of the walls.

Include symbols for light fixtures, outlets, and heat registers. Note load-bearing walls, which cannot be moved without compromising structural integrity. If you are thinking about tearing out any wall and you don't know whether it is load-bearing, consult an architect.

It's a good idea to list your gripes about the old kitchen on the sketch, too. That way you can see at a glance what problems exist and which ones you want to change.

Remember: this floor plan doesn't have to be professionally drawn, only accurate in its rendition of the current kitchen space. Before you proceed, check and then double-check your measurements to ensure accuracy.

configuring space

Whether you are reconfiguring existing space or adding on, the floor plan plays a large role in how well the room will function. And while a kitchen addition to an outside wall of the house offers the best possibilities for unencumbered floor space, it is the costliest option. One way to save money is to restrict your addition to a "bump-out" of 3 feet or less. This doesn't necessarily require a new foundation, and it limits the need for a new roof. Consult an architect or builder, first, to make sure the existing structure is sound and can carry the additional structural load. Remember to inquire about local zoning ordinances that may affect your design before going ahead with plans or construction.

However you choose to proceed, a kitchen of any size requires a thoughtful arrangement of all its elements to make it both highly functional and efficient.

Work Zones

Almost everybody has heard of the kitchen's classic work triangle. Essentially, it is an area that puts the three major work centers—the range, refrigerator, and sink—at the three points of a triangle. The spatial relationship among these sites and how they relate to other areas in the kitchen are what makes the room an efficient work space. In the classic work triangle, the distance between any pair of the three centers is no longer than nine feet and no less than four feet.

To conserve walking distance from point to point without sacrificing adequate counter space, the sum of all three lines of the triangle should be no greater than 26 feet and no less than 12 feet. For a large kitchen, plan two or more work triangles. Although pairs may extend inside one another, sharing one side or "leg" of the triangle for maximum performance, do not overlap the sink and range areas. An alternative is to design two or more small triangles (work zones) set within one large triangle.

The National Kitchen & Bath Association (NKBA) recommends there be at least one work triangle in a kitchen. In fact, today's busy families—and multipurpose kitchens—often call for two or more separate work triangles. With traditional roles at home changing, so are attitudes about cooking. Two-cook families are more common than ever, and food preparation and cooking have themselves become reasons for social events where

even the guests actively participate and everybody helps with the cleanup.

Because a goal of the work triangle is to keep normal kitchen traffic from interrupting the work flow, during your planning stage pay especially close attention to how everyone in the household comes and goes in the existing layout. You might even try this admittedly unusual but enlightening homespun experiment: dust the floor with a thin coating of cornmeal; then go about your normal food preparation and cleanup routine. You'll be able to track your movements from cabinets to appliances to sink and the rest of the family's moves around you—or whoever does the cooking. Once you see where the kitchen becomes most crowded, you'll be able to make the necessary changes. (And don't forget to thoroughly sweep up the cornmeal afterward!) Sometimes that's as simple as relocating an appliance—particularly a small one like the microwave—to a less-busy area. For ideas, take a look at the floor plan examples of typical kitchen traffic problems and their solutions, which appear on the next two pages.

There is some debate, today, among professional kitchen designers concerning the traditional work triangle. Although most agree that it is still an important element, many see the triangular space evolving as cooking habits and lifestyles change. These designers feel that the more actual living done in

ABOVE **This design of a work triangle demonstrates good distance limits between the three primary work centers—the range, or cooktop, the refrigerator, and the sink. A larger triangle would require too much walking; a smaller one would create a cramped layout.**

the kitchen, the more expanded the basic triangle will have to become. And as kitchens grow larger—which appears to be the trend—they will embrace an increasing number of activities. This will result in the need for several autonomous triangles within the room. Whichever school of thought you follow, the bottom line still is and always will be: design for your sake, not for the sake of design.

Adding On

If reorganizing existing space isn't enough, you may have to build an addition. Adding on will raise your budget significantly; it requires excavating and laying a new foundation and installing new plumbing, electrical, and mechanical systems. You may have to supplement or replace your heating system to handle the new load. And you will definitely have to extend the roof. This is a major undertaking.

If reconfiguring your existing space won't solve the problem and the thought of adding on is too daunting or more than you can afford, consider some other options:

■ **Steal Space.** Look at adjacent spaces, such as hallways, pantries, under the stairs, or even an adjoining room. You may be able to open up the layout or create enough floor space to accommodate an island or peninsula by removing a non-load-bearing wall.

■ **Recess Appliances and Cabinets.** You can set custom cabinets as much as 6 inches into the wall between wall studs. Why not do the same for appliances? This doesn't sound like much of a space gain, but 6 inches on each side of a room may yield enough additional square footage for an efficient work triangle.

■ **Convert.** Don't limit your search for extra space to the interior living areas of your house. Take over the garage or the back porch. Although you'll have to weatherize them, that project is

considerably less expensive than building an addition.

Revisit your original base plan and, using a different color, pencil in possible convertible or attachable space.

■ **Relocate.** Have you thought about moving the kitchen to another location in the house? Is there a dining room or bedroom on the ground floor you aren't using? This type of remodeling, while perhaps more extensive and more expensive than stealing space from an adjacent room, could be far less costly than building an addition.

ABOVE
If you plan to add on space for a new kitchen, you might want to hire an architect to be sure the new structure integrates with the existing house.

Before

After

Sink   Base Cabinets   Wall Cabinets

Dining Room

Refrigerator

Range

Closet

Sink

Range

Refrigerator

Closet   Closet

ABOVE Doors at opposite corners created diagonal traffic that cut off the range from the sink and refrigerator areas (left). Moving both doors pulls traffic out of the work zone (right). The U-shaped layout puts the refrigerator, sink, and range in a good working arrangement.

Before

After

Breakfast Bar

Sink

Range

Back Hall

Dining Room

Refrigerator

Breakfast Bar

Sink

Range

Refrigerator

Dining Room

Planning Desk

Back Hall

ABOVE Open kitchens can have traffic problems, too. Here, the refrigerator is isolated, away from the sink and range, and the work area sprawls over a kitchen with too many doors (left). Moving one door and closing another gets traffic out of the work zone (right). Relocating the range makes the breakfast bar much more usable.

Before

After

ABOVE Old-fashioned kitchens often failed to provide a place to set down food near the refriger-ator. Again, traffic interrupts the work zone. Shifting the doorway redirects traffic and allows for more counter and storage space.

creating a layout

All you may be thinking of doing is updating appliances, replacing cabinetry, and installing new flooring, countertops, and wallpaper. But you may want to think about modifying the layout, at least on paper. During these preliminary phases, you have nothing to lose by playing with the idea. You may be surprised to see how much a few minor changes in your floor plan can improve your original layout. Would the space function better if you moved a doorway or perhaps added or eliminated a window? As long as you're not moving or adding gas or electrical supply lines, your changes may not be terribly complicated. Try sketching different arrangements to see how they would work. Would the layout improve if you could move the gas line for the range, or scoot plumbing lines over a foot or two? While structural and service changes such as these certainly do add to the cost of the remodel, they could also be money well spent if they result in a kitchen that is more functional on a day-to-day basis for years to come.

smart tip CORNERS

One of the trickiest parts of planning a run of cabinets and appliances comes when you arrive at a corner. There are ways to negotiate this with cabinetry. The two most popular and efficient ones are a blind base—a straight unit with a door on only one side that overlaps the beginning of the next run—or a corner base, which integrates two cabinets into a single L-shaped unit. With blind bases you usually need a filler so that doors will clear each other. Wall cabinets also come in blind and corner units.

Another way to negotiate a turn is with a sink, refrigerator, or range. Corner sinks may arrange basins at right angles to each other and fit into a standard corner base. Allow adequate counter space on either side.

A peninsula will let you take advantage of dead corner space in cabinets. Like blind bases, peninsula corner cabinets come in left- and right-hand configurations.

smart steps
plan like the pros

■ **Step 1** MAKE A NEW BASE DRAWING

As with the base drawing you made for the old kitchen, use a ½-inch scale. If you are using a ¼-inch grid, each square would then represent a 6-inch square of real floor space. Begin by drawing the outer walls, and then add the windows and doors.

■ **Step 2** MAKE TEMPLATES OF THE APPLIANCES AND CABINETS

Paper templates of appliances and cabinets are an easy way to experiment with different layouts, or you can purchase manufactured design kits or easy-to-use software packages. Otherwise, refer to the Appendix at the back of this book, where you will find templates of typical-size cabinets, appliances, and sinks, which you can trace. Cut them out so you can move them around your plan. If you have collected spec sheets (printed product information from manufacturers) for the items you may be purchasing, use the supplied dimensions to create your own templates to scale.

■ **Step 3** PLACE THE APPLIANCES, FIXTURES, AND CABINETRY

You will use some appliances more often than others: first the sink, next the range, then the refrigerator. Create your work triangles initially, and then specify storage cabinets and counters around them. Indicate all windows and doors; also measure and note the door swing.

Once you have your work triangles arranged, locate auxiliary features, such as the dishwasher, microwave, trash compactor, indoor grill, and oven. If there is

any leeway in the plan, place the oven so it doesn't open near a door in into a busy traffic aisle. If possible, do the same for the dishwasher and refrigerator. Don't forget to pencil in all the cabinetry—both upper and lower—as well as an island or peninsula or special built-in units such as a desk or pantry. Be sure to include the dining table in an eat-in kitchen and any other freestanding furnishings you expect to use.

Pay particular attention to point-of-use storage. Specify a place to keep spices, pots, and pans near the cooktop; dry goods like flour and sugar at the bake center; and paper and plasticware near the microwave.

A different but valid approach is to place big items first. Start with any large commercial appliances, if you have them, and then work down in size to the small items, which might include the trash compactor or recycling bins.

A lot of what you will do is just common sense, such as keeping the dishwasher and refrigerator near the sink for easy cooking and cleanup. If you have

ABOVE **Because it is typically narrow, a galley (or corridor-style) kitchen works best for one cook at a time. You should allow for a 48-in.-wide aisle, but you can cut it down to 36 in. if space is really at a premium.**

space for two or more work triangles with separate sinks, reserve one for the food preparation area and the other for the cleanup zone.

Although function must be uppermost in your mind when designing a kitchen layout, don't forget about aesthetics. Remember the sight lines from outside the room when situating a work zone or a high-traffic area, as well as large appliances such as the sink, stove, and refrigerator. And try to keep the cleanup as far from view from the living area as possible. As you

draw your layout, apply the principles of balance and symmetry whenever possible. Center the sink under a window or on a wall, for example.

Most of all, remember front and side clearances when locating appliances and permanent fixtures. This ensures that all doors and drawers will be operable. Codes usually require a minimum clearance for each one. Check with your local building department, and ask about regulations for the placement of electrical outlets and appliances, too.

ABOVE **A kitchen that is configured along one wall requires the least amount of space. To maximize accessibility and allow for two people to use the kitchen at once, place the sink between the cooktop or range and refrigerator.**

Basic Kitchen Layouts

There are five basic kitchen layouts: one-wall, galley (corridor-style; see page 44), U-shaped, L-shaped, and G-shaped. Each has its challenges and advantages.

■ **One-Wall.** This arrangement places all the equipment, sink, and cabinetry along one wall. Because you cannot create a triangle in a one-wall kitchen, maximize accessibility by locating the sink between the refrigerator and the range. Although a one-wall kitchen is more typical in a small apartment, it may be found in a large, open-plan home. If you want to retain this arrangement but would like to close off the kitchen from other public areas of the house, install sliding doors or screens that can be opened or closed at will. Or, if there's enough space in an open plan, consider adding a half wall with a built-in eating bar opposite the wall with the appliances. If you relocate an appliance or sink to this side, you've created a galley-style layout, which is discussed next.

ABOVE **A U-shaped design is generally considered the most efficient layout in the least amount of space and provides the greatest amount of counter space between the sink and appliances.**

■ **The Galley.** Also known as the corridor style, this compact layout locates the appliances, sink, and cabinets on two parallel walls to create a small pass-through kitchen. It's easy to configure an efficient work triangle in this setup, but this layout really caters to one cook. Allow a 48-inch-wide aisle after all fixtures are in place so that cabinet and appliance doors can be opened easily while someone walks through. If space is really tight, you could make the aisle 36 inches wide, but appliance doors may collide with each other if more than one is open at the same time. Another tip: avoid installing doorways at both ends of the galley or corridor. That way, you can keep people from walking through the work triangle while the cook is busy.

To ease as many traffic problems as possible, place the refrigerator near the end of a galley kitchen—away from the entrance into the room. Another option is to install the primary refrigerator in the food preparation area and a small model for soft drinks or snacks close to the doorway.

Storage is a real challenge in this compact layout. The solution is to install tall cabinets that extend to the ceiling. You'll have to keep a stepladder handy for gaining access to what's on top, so reserve that space for items that you don't use often but want to store in the kitchen.

■ **The U-shape.** Some experts believe the U-shaped kitchen is the most efficient design, but others say it's a matter of personal preference. Cabinets, counters, and appliances are all arranged along three walls in a U configuration. The greatest

In an L-shaped kitchen, two intersecting walls are put to work. You can often fit a table or booth into the corner by placing it diagonally opposite the L.

Two cooks can easily maneuver around a G-shaped layout, which surrounds you with work space, offering enough room for two work triangles. Both of them are typically anchored at the refrigerator.

benefit to this plan is the easy traffic flow. Generally speaking, in a U-shaped kitchen it's possible to keep traffic that's passing through the kitchen from encroaching on the cook's work space, an important asset in a busy household.

A U-shaped layout incorporates a logical sequence of work centers with minimum distances between each. The sink is often located at the base of the U, with the refrigerator and range on the side walls opposite each other. The U shape takes a lot of space—at least 8 feet along the length and width of the kitchen. Corners may be a problem because they often create unusable space. However, you can overcome that by angling cabinets into otherwise "dead" areas. Corner units on the countertop make roomy appliance garages, and bottom cabinets with carousel shelves or Lazy Susans actually make storage more handy than standard units.

Smaller U-shaped kitchens can be dark because of the sheer mass of all that cabinetry. You can overcome this drawback with a generous-size window, skylights, or under-cabinet task lighting, or by keeping surfaces a light color.

The U-shaped kitchen is ideal for two cooks and two work triangles. The work areas may have to overlap somewhat in a smaller layout—meaning two cooks may have to share one leg of the triangle—but it can be done.

■ **The L-shape.** This plan places the kitchen on two perpendicular walls. The L-shape usually consists of one long and one short "leg," and lends itself to an efficient work triangle

without the problem of through traffic. If it's well designed, it's flexible enough for two cooks to work simultaneously without getting in each other's way.

Another advantage to this layout is the opportunity for incorporating an island into the floor plan, if space allows. (Attach a peninsula to one leg of the design, and you've created an F-shaped space.) If you do include an island or peninsula in an L-shaped kitchen, plan the clearances carefully. Walkways should be at least 36 inches wide. If the walkway is also a work aisle, increase the clearance to 42 inches. A 36-inch clearance is fine for counter seating, unless traffic goes behind it. In that case, clearance should be 65 inches, to allow sufficient space for people to pass behind any already seated diners.

■ **The G-shape.** This is a hybrid of the U-shape with a shorter, fourth leg added in the form of a peninsula. While the G-shaped layout is suitable for more than one person working in the kitchen, it may feel confining—particularly with an island located in the center.

This layout may feature a pair of sinks and a separate cooktop, as well as oven ranges. One work triangle usually incorporates a sink, the cooktop, and the refrigerator, while the other houses the second sink, the oven, and, overlapping the first triangle, the refrigerator.

The G-shaped kitchen easily accommodates specialty appliances, such as warming drawers, modular refrigeration, or a built-in grill, to allow independence between the two work areas.

Islands and Peninsulas

In a roomy layout, you can shorten the distance between the three key work areas by adding an island or peninsula. A peninsula base and ceiling-hung cabinets offer convenient storage for tableware and linens. In an L- or U-shaped kitchen, an island can add visual interest, breaking up the space without confining it. It also provides an extra work surface, a convenient spot for snacks or informal meals, as well as a place for setting up a buffet when entertaining.

An island or peninsula can also serve as an excellent location for a cooktop or second sink, if plumbing and ventilation hookups permit. It could also prove the ideal spot for a wine rack or cooler, a wet bar, warming drawers, modular refrigerator units, or additional general storage. For maximum efficiency, be sure the design provides a clearance of 48 inches from the island or peninsula to the wall cabinets.

Eating Areas

There are specific minimum clearances you'll need to accommodate a table and chairs, which you must not forget to include in a design for an eat-in kitchen. Plan enough floor space for all the furniture and for people to sit down, get up, and walk around the table comfortably, without interfering with the work traffic.

Seating Allowances. If you feel as if you're a contortionist every time you get into or out of your chair at the table, the person who designed the existing kitchen didn't do proper space-planning homework. When you redesign, follow the guidelines here and you won't go wrong.

Even average-size people need a surprising amount of space to make a dining area accessible. Allow 12 to 15 square feet per person. That means a family of four will require at least 48 square feet in an eat-in kitchen. Assume that a 36-inch-diameter round table can seat four adults; a 48-inch-diameter one will accommodate six. Calculate 21 to 24 inches of table space per person for a square or rectangular table.

When planning space for your kitchen table, pay attention to the distance between it and the walls or cabinets. A seated adult occupies a depth of about 20 inches from the edge of the table but will need 12 to 16 additional inches of space to push back the chair and rise. This means you have to plan on 32 to 36 inches of clearance between the wall and the edge of the table. You can get away with a minimum of 28 inches if chairs are angled to the wall. However, plan on a 44-inch clearance to allow enough room on any serving side of any table, whatever its shape.

If you don't have enough room for a table, a booth or a table with banquette, or bench, seating may be the answer. A kitchen alcove or bay window offers a natural spot for this type of seating arrangement, or you can back it against an island, peninsula, or wall. Plan 21 inches of table space for each person, with at least 15 inches of knee space underneath. This means that a family of four minimally needs a 42-inch-long table that measures 30 inches across. Because you slide in and out of a booth, the table may overhang the benches by 3 or 4 inches. Total floor space required for a four-person booth, therefore, measures only 5 feet across, compared with a minimum requirement of about 9 feet for a freestanding table with chairs.

Another popular option for in-kitchen dining is to let the island or peninsula serve double duty as an eating bar. Remember, each adult requires at least 21 inches of table space, so that means a 63-inch-long counter (a typical size) will accommodate three stools at most.

Seating depends on counter height. A 28- to 32-inch-high counter requires 18-inch-high chairs with 20 inches of knee space under the bar. If you make the island or peninsula the same height as the rest of the kitchen countertops (36 inches being the standard), you'll be able to accommodate 24-inch-high stools and 14 inches of knee space. Go up to bar height (42 to 45 inches), and you'll need 30-inch-high stools with footrests, also with 14 inches of knee space.

Secondary Work Centers

One of the most popular secondary work centers in new kitchens today is the home office. You may place it in another part of the room—away from food preparation tasks—and include a desk, bookcase, and accommodations for a computer, printer, phone, and fax machine. Or you may want to incorporate it in the main area as part of the built-in cabinetry. That's fine, as long as it's outside the work triangles. If the work surface and storage are designed as part of the kitchen cabinetry, you'll have to drop the counter height to about 30 inches to be comfortable sitting there. If you're purchasing stock cabinets, you should be able to buy 30-inch-high base units for areas that adjoin the desk. These can be used to house supplies and files. Keep the depth of your desk the same as the rest of the countertops so you have one smooth line of cabinetry, but be sure there is a comfortable amount of knee space (approximately 15 inches) underneath.

Serious craft devotees can follow the same advice when planning their hobby work space. Incorporating a roll-top counter appliance garage with an electrical outlet in the design allows you to store a portable sewing machine or other heavy equipment, so you won't have to lift it onto the desk or countertop.

Another specialty area desired by serious cooks, especially bakers, is a bake center. For this space, allocate at least 36 inches near the oven or refrigerator, ideally between the two appliances. Specify 30-inch-high base cabinets, which are a more comfortable height for mixing and kneading. An extra-deep countertop (30 inches or more) will provide plenty of room for rolling out dough.

Gardening enthusiasts may also appreciate a dedicated area away from the bustle of food preparation and cleanup. Equipped with its own sink—and perhaps a window—this space might include a cabinet and drawers to house containers and vases, tools, plant food, and other related items. A convenient arrangement is a counter that measures 36 inches high and a tall chair or stool with 12 inches of knee space.

Locating laundry facilities in the kitchen can be tricky unless you have lots of floor space. Like other appliances with doors, washers and dryers in use can tangle traffic aisles. Another complication: your washer will most probably have to be placed next to, if not nearby, a sink. If you don't have the room to park these machines in a separate but adjacent nook off the kitchen or in a bathroom, and you don't want to haul dirty laundry to the basement, be sure to place these workhorse appli-

ances thoughtfully. A side-by-side pair of full-size appliances measures 48 to 58 inches in width. Full-size units are also about 6 inches taller than typical counter heights. If you're really pressed for floor space, you might want to think about stackable washer and dryer models.

Once you conclude how you want your new kitchen space to function, you're in a position to tackle the challenge: selecting products, materials, and cabinetry.

smart tip ISLAND DREAM

These days it seems just about every kitchen features an island. However, an island isn't always the right solution, and, in fact, can present problems in a space that's just too small to accommodate it. Give up your dreams of an island if the space does not allow for the minimum clearances on all sides. These vary from 36"-65" and depend on function and layout. Also, make sure those clearances are not compromised by opening a nearby appliance or cabinet door.

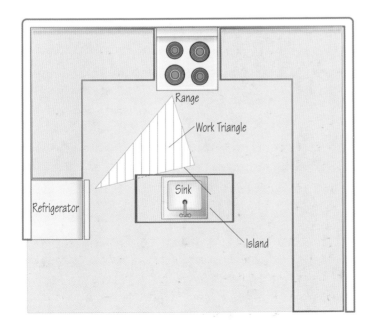

ABOVE Depending on the location of utility lines and venting possibilities, either the sink or cooktop can be installed into a kitchen island.

ABOVE A peninsula brings counter space and storage conveniently close without interfering with the work triangle. It works well with an L-shaped layout.

design workbook

THE GALLEY KITCHEN

bright and efficient

This compact and efficient galley kitchen offers all the major components within steps of each other. Note that the large window and light-color surfaces help to keep the space bright.

dine in

There's sufficient space for locating a family-sized dining area just beyond the work space. (See also top left.)

use every inch

Open metal shelving provides storage for frequently used items in this galley kitchen. Task lighting illuminates the counters (far left).

keep it simple

Light monochromatic floors and walls help to visually stretch small space. Contemporary compact strip lighting provide a touch of drama and style. (See also left.)

design workbook
THE ONE-WALL KITCHEN

room for two

The function of this commodious one-wall kitchen, which offers plenty of countertop work space for two cooks, is further improved by the addition of a large triangular island.

pull it together

Visually unite the island and the main work wall by using identical cabinets, countertop and backsplash material, and light fixtures in both areas. (See also top left.)

add function

A multifunctional island separates the work area of the kitchen from adjoining living spaces and provides a spot for casual dining or for guests to perch while visiting with the cook. Adding another sink creates a galley latout and allows the island to function as a bar and a second work zone. (See also left.)

design workbook

THE U-SHAPED KITCHEN

gathering space

A generous island is the central spot for informal gathering and an extra work space. (See also left.)

large-scale style

In a kitchen meant for entertaining, a pair of wrought-iron chandeliers adds Old World sophistication.

cooking smarts

A commercial cooktop and custom range hood is recessed into an alcove across from the island (below far left).

customized cooling

Upscale refrigeration is concealed inside custom cabinetry at the far end of the work aisle. (See also left.)

personality plus

For visual interest, the cooking alcove is set apart with red laminate countertops. (See also middle left.)

design workbook

THE G-SHAPED KITCHEN

expansive counters

One of the main advantages of a G-shaped kitchen, with its trademark peninsula, is the generous expanse of contiguous countertops. A terra cotta-color tile backsplash and well-placed accent lighting warm up the look of all-white cabinetry.

built-in eat-in space

The overhang on the peninsula top is wide and deep enough for casual dining space for four. Note the location of the desk, which allows the family message center to reside in the heart of the home, but still out of the way. (See also top left.)

storage specifics

Storage for the preparation and cleanup areas is located at one end of the space and balanced by storage for items such as wine and tableware at the other end (left).

design workbook

SECONDARY WORK CENTERS

entertaining ideas

With furniture-like details this open-plan kitchen is designed as the center of many social gatherings, especially at the elegantly appointed island.

hidden asset

Cabinetry extends to an enclosure for the cooktop's exhaust system (top left).

butler's pantry

An adjacent butler's pantry has extra storage. It's fitted with a wine refrigerator, too. (See also below far left.)

easy access

A microwave, tucked into the end of the island across from the snack bar, is set at an easily accessed height (middle left).

snack center

A snack center next to the refrigerator and near the microwave has a handy second sink. (See also left.)

easy does it

SAFETY   UNIVERSAL DESIGN   ADAPTABLE DESIGN   ACCESSIBLE DESIGN

By the year 2020 more than 20 percent of the American population will be over the age of 65, according to the United States Census Bureau. Some of these people will suffer disabilities that limit their sight, hearing, or mobility. Universal design addresses their needs, as well as those of multigenerational households. As Baby Boomers bring home their aging parents while raising families of their own, it is not uncommon to have young children and grandparents living under one roof. Indeed, as our population ages it benefits everyone to think about ways to make the kitchen functional—and safe—for every member of the family. Manufacturers of cabinets and appliances are also taking this into account when they design their new products. In this chapter, you'll find out what you can do to make your kitchen universally appealing.

Incorporate universal design principles into your new kitchen to ensure that all family members can use the space with equal ease.

More building codes govern the kitchen than any other room in the house. That's because so many accidents occur there. Think about it: sharp knives; intense heat; electrical appliances in close proximity to water; hard, unforgiving surfaces; breakable glassware and china. These are some of the ingredients in a perfect recipe for kitchen accidents. They also represent safety concerns that should be considered during the design stage. Although this is true under any circumstances, it is particularly important when those who will be using the kitchen are the most vulnerable: children and the elderly. With that in mind, safety should reign as a primary factor in any kitchen remodel. Your goal should be to lessen the chance of injury while increasing the performance of what is probably the most popular room in your house.

Take the following steps when designing for safety. And remember: you don't have to be very young or very old to suffer an injury in the kitchen. One of the most common Sunday morning hospital emergency room visits is by someone who has sliced open a hand while cutting a bagel.

smart steps
safety

■ Step 1 USE PROPER LIGHTING

Never work in a dim space. Good general lighting, supplemented with proper task lighting clearly focused on a work surface, without glare or shadows, can vastly decrease your chance of injury while preparing a meal. In addition, good lighting should be adaptable to meet the needs of younger, as well as older, eyes. Review Chapter Seven, "Lighting The Kitchen," beginning on page 148, for specific advice regarding how much light you need and where it should be placed.

■ Step 2 USE SLIP-RESISTANT FLOORING

Falling with a hot casserole or sharp knife in your hand can have serious consequences. Choose a slip-resistant material for your floor, such as matte-finished wood or laminate, textured vinyl, or a soft-glazed ceramic tile indicated specifically for flooring. If you select tile, it helps to use a throw rug with a non-skid backing—especially around areas that get wet. When you're shopping, remember to inquire about the slip-resistance rating of any flooring material you may be considering for your new kitchen.

Step 3 KEEP A FIRE EXTINGUISHER HANDY

A grease fire in the kitchen can spread rapidly. That's why it's so important to have a fire extinguisher within arm's reach of the ovens and cooktop. For maximum protection, there should be at least two extinguishers in any kitchen—one located in the cooking area and one stored in another part of the room. You want them to be handy; however, you don't want fire extinguishers to fall into the hands of children. Install them high enough so that they are safely out of the reach of curious youngsters.

Step 4 ELECTRICAL SWITCHES

Keep plugs and lighting fixtures away from water sources and wet hands. In addition, make sure every electrical receptacle is grounded and protected with ground-fault circuit interrupters. These important devices cut electrical current if there is a power surge or if moisture is present. Most building codes require them where there is plumbing to protect homeowners against electrical shock.

Step 5 CONSIDER LOCK-OUT OPTIONS

New smart-home technology allows you to lock your range and ovens so that no one can use them while you are out of the house. The simple lock-out device can prevent burns, fires, or worse. You can choose between lock-out covers or a programmed lock-out system. Or you can install timers on all appliances you don't want in use when you can't supervise the cooking. Installing guard rails around burners is another good idea.

Step 6 REGULATE WATER TEMPERATURE

Install faucets with antiscald devices that prevent water temperature from rising too high, or buy pressure-balanced valves that equalize hot and cold water.

OPPOSITE
A sharp contrast in the color of surfaces, such as between countertops and flooring, makes the kitchen easier for all to use.

ABOVE
Good task lighting that properly illuminates work surfaces will help to prevent accidents.

RIGHT
Provide electrical switches and outlets where they are safe and convenient to work zones.

Although pressure-balanced faucets were available only in single-lever styles in the past, now some models with separate hot- and cold-water valves offer this safety feature, too. Another option is a faucet that can be preprogrammed to your desired temperature setting. All of these controls should be childproofed with lock-out features.

Step 7 DESIGN A SAFE COOKTOP

How many times have you been scalded reaching over a boiling pot or a hot element? Avoid this dangerous situation by selecting staggered burners for your cook-top or one straight row of burners. If you can't find sin-

gle burners, turn two-burner units sideways, placing them parallel to the front of the countertop. Never choose a unit with controls at the rear of the cooktop; controls should be along the side or in front. Again, if you live with small children, opt for a lockout feature for knobs and controls. Finally, plan proper illumination above the cooktop surface. One easy way to do this is to choose a range hood that includes built-in halogen or incandescent lighting.

Step 8 USE SPACE EFFICIENTLY AND SAFELY

You can have all the space in the world and still put family members in compromising situations. Avoid using swinging doors within the kitchen space. If you must use a door that swings, be sure it incorporates a safety glass window so you can see if there is anyone on the other side. When locating appliances within the new plan, think about how the traffic area will be affected when the oven, refrigerator, or dishwasher doors are open. Locate ovens and the microwave at a comfortable height that doesn't necessitate over-reaching in order to retrieve hot food. Install carousel shelves, Lazy Susans, and slide-out trays and bins in base cabinets to make storage more accessible without doing a lot of bending.

Avoid sharp corners on countertop edges, especially at the end of a run of cabinetry or on the island or peninsula. While this is more comfortable for anyone who might bump into the edge, it's especially important if you share your home with small children. If space is tight and you can't rearrange most elements, install a rounded end cabinet and choose a countertop material that will allow a bull-nose edge treatment. Solid-surfacing material is an excellent choice for such an application. Granite and other natural stones can be finished to a soft curved edge.

OPPOSITE
Store heavy objects on shelves and in drawers that correspond to the area between your shoulders and knees.

ABOVE LEFT
Locate the microwave at a height to suit the primary users. Make sure it is installed so that users are not required to reach over-head to retrieve hot dishes.

LEFT
Slide-out bins and cabinets let you retrieve items with ease.

universal design

As people age, their capabilities change; some become more challenged than others and need more assistance with day-to-day chores. Universal design is an approach that adapts the home to people of all skills. It evolved as a response to our increasingly aging society.

Incorporating universal design into your remodeling is always smart, particularly if you plan to stay in your house as you grow older. Analyze your lifestyle and your family's needs now—and what you anticipate them to be in the future. Do you have young children? Do you expect to have an elderly parent living with you? Will you remain in the house after you retire? Planning to include some universal-design features in your new kitchen now will save you money later on, because it's more expensive to make changes to an existing plan.

According to the National Kitchen & Bath Association (NKBA), one of the easiest and most practical universal-design elements you can include is the installation of counters at varying heights, which allows you to perform some tasks while seated and others while standing, not bending. Another idea that makes sense for any kitchen is a pullout counter near the cooktop and another at the oven. They provide handy landing places for hot pots, pans, and dishes. Or design a compact work

OPPOSITE
Plan countertops at varied heights so that each family member can find a comfortable spot for working.

ABOVE LEFT
Many people find that a dishwasher is more comfortable to load when it's installed a foot or so above floor level.

ABOVE RIGHT
A compact work area saves the cook many steps.

triangle that eliminates the need for extra steps. For most people, an L-shaped layout accomplishes this most efficiently. (See Chapter Two, "Choose a Layout," beginning on page 30.)

Other ideas include digital displays, which are easier to read and fairly standard on today's appliances; wall-mounted switches and outlets at the universal reach range of 15 to 48 inches from the floor; reserving a base cabinet for dishes, making dinnerware easier to reach; wrist-blade-style faucets that don't require grabbing or twisting; and a side-by-side style refrigerator, which places most foods at accessible heights.

It might also be worthwhile to investigate some of the smart-home technology available. This includes devices that allow you to call home from any phone to turn on the lights, heat the oven, raise the thermostat, or program dinner to start cooking. Of course, this sophisticated technology is expensive and may be more practical for new construction; some things are too complicated to retrofit into an existing home. If any of these features will destroy your budget, don't use them.

smart tip

BE PREPARED

It's not just those with permanent physical limitations who can benefit from incorporating the features of universal design into a kitchen. Well-placed light switches and appliance controls, adequate task lighting, and a countertop that permits the cook to sit while working, all add optimal function every day. And should you or a family member be side-lined with even a temporary injury or illness, the kitchen remains accessible.

You may have heard the terms accessible and adaptable design used interchangeably and with universal design. However, all of these are different. You've just learned about universal design; here's an explanation of the other two.

Accessible Design

Accessible design normally means that a home—or in this case a kitchen—is barrier-free. It also indicates that the room complies with design guidelines for disabled people found in government regulations such as the American National Standards Institute's A117.1 (ANSI A117.1-1986). There are a number of guidelines governing accessible design, the goal of which is to provide criteria for designing for the wheelchair-bound. Most accessible homes incorporate a number of fixed features that give a disabled person easy access.

If a disabled person in your family will use the new kitchen, plan the space accordingly, making sure there is adequate room for that person to move around. Design appropriate clearances. A standard wheelchair occupies 10 square feet and has a turning diameter of 5 feet. Therefore, doorways must be at least 32 inches wide, and aisles must be a minimum of 42 inches wide, according to the NKBA.

A lowered cooktop with an angled nonfogging mirror installed above the surface lets someone seated see what's cooking. If you don't like the look of an open space below the cooktop, install retractable doors that open to accommodate the wheelchair and close for a finished look. An induction cooktop is probably the most practical choice for this situation. It features an automatic shutoff, has a cool-to-the-touch cooking surface, and is easy to keep clean. Low, shallow base cabinets outfitted with pullout and slide-out bins and trays, carousel shelves, and Lazy Susans maximize accessibility, as do lower counter heights—31 inches as opposed to the standard 36 inches. Light-colored countertops with a contrasting edge treatment are recommended for people with impaired vision.

More than one cabinet manufacturer has introduced a line of cabinets and accessories that accommodate everyone in the family, including those with special needs. Features include a lowered base cabinet; an oven cabinet accessible from a seated position; a raised dishwasher enclosure for easy loading and unloading; a sink base that allows seated use but conceals plumbing; a 9-inch-deep toekick to permit wheelchair access; a tambour-door base cabinet unit; base microwave cabinets; and knife hinges for barrier-free door opening. Each one of these features reflects an idea that should be designed into any all-accessible kitchen.

You might also want to consider having a second microwave near the kitchen table. The cabinet in which you choose to house it should have a drop-down door to provide a shelf for resting hot dishes straight from the oven.

And if you have the space, keep one or two rolling carts in the kitchen that allow someone to easily transport several items around the room—especially foods on large serving platters—at the same time.

Adaptable Design

Adaptable design refers to features that can be easily modified for use by a disabled person. Such design features are normally found in multifamily rental housing so that a landlord is able to rent to anyone. The adaptable-design kitchen incorporates some concealed traditional accessible features—for example, doors under the sink that can be removed to allow accessibility for someone in a wheelchair.

RIGHT
The raised dishwasher, varied countertop height, and the eye-level placement of the microwave eliminate back strain for the cook in this kitchen.

smart tip OUTLETS AND SWITCHES

Sometimes the needs of those with certain physical limitations may seem to conflict with those of the very young. A case in point is accessible light switch and electrical outlet placement. The limited reach of a small-stature adult or an adult in a wheelchair demands that light switches and other electrical controls need to be placed low down on the wall. While this is safe and convenient for the adult, it could put electrical devices within easy reach of small children.

As an alternative that meets the needs of both groups, the NKBA recommends locating electrical control switches and outlets just inside the front of a tilt-down drawer. This technique conceals them from children, but leaves them easily accessible to adults. Alternatively, an outlet strip can be kept out of a child's reach and at a convenient location that lessens the distance the adult must reach to access plugs and switches installed in the backsplash.

design workbook
UNIVERSAL DESIGN IS FOR ALL

unobstructed aisle

Be sure that appliance and cabinet doors can open fully without obstructing the flow of foot traffic.

reachable switches

Install light switches and receptacles at convenient locations all around the kitchen (top left).

task lighting

Illuminate areas where knives and other kitchen tools will be used by adding undercabinet light fixtures. (See also far left.)

cabinet pull handles

Choose decorative cabinet hardware pulls that are large enough to grasp comfortably without catching fingers. (See also left.)

rounded edges

Prevent eye injuries for kids and bruises and bumps for adults with softly rounded corners on countertops. (See also left.)

4

the best materials

COUNTERTOPS   FLOORING   SINKS, FAUCETS, AND MORE
DESIGN WORKBOOKS

Take the stress out of selecting materials and products for your new kitchen by getting to know the latest and best offerings on the market. Some shoppers select their new products based on efficiency, some for their design, and some for the price. Remember, however, that top-of-the-line materials usually come for top dollar. Factors that influence the cost of new appliances, cabinetry, countertops, and flooring include updated technology and the type of finish. The smarter the device, the more you'll pay for it. Likewise, the fancier the finish, the higher the price tag. But cost doesn't always reflect quality, nor does it promise satisfaction. It's not always about how much you can spend but how realistic you are about what you need. Is one countertop material or flooring type really any better than another? Yes and no.

Gorgeous granite is one of the costliest countertop materials. Is it worth it? It will probably outlast everything else in the kitchen.

How can you tell whether a product is reliable, whether it will endure and take daily abuse? To find out, comparison shop, and don't be afraid to ask questions. Otherwise, you'll have to take your chances. If you're not the gambling type, however, here are steps you can take to select products and materials with confidence.

smart steps
be particular

Step 1 SEPARATE PRODUCT FROM HYPE

A high price tag doesn't always mean high quality. Find out what's different about one refrigerator that costs $1,000 and another that sells for $7,000. (See Chapter Six: "Choosing Appliances," beginning on page 116.) That way you can decide whether the higher-priced model is worth it. A knowledgeable salesperson will be able to tell you. If not, contact the manufacturer. Many have toll-free phone numbers and Web sites set up to answer consumer questions. Sometimes the high price is because of a feature you can't see. For example, a faucet with replaceable parts costs much more than one with parts that can't be replaced. How much do you want to gamble that the faucet won't break?

Step 2 WEIGH YOUR OPTIONS

Analyze the pros and cons that come with each product. Once you have that information, reaching a decision will be easier. For example, if you are sprucing up an old kitchen or adding a new one in a house you expect to sell soon, you might install a less-expensive countertop material. But if you are making a major investment in a remodeling project that you plan to live with for a long time, you will be happier in the long run with an item that may cost more but will give you great satisfaction and be reliable for years to come.

Step 3 SEEK SOUND ADVICE

Ask the manufacturer about the expected lifespan of the product and its efficiency. Don't take advice from a store clerk if he or she is not an experienced remodeling professional. Talk to your contractor. He may be familiar with the product or can pass along critical feedback about it from other clients.

Step 4 STYLE OR COLOR CHOICES

It doesn't work for cars, and it won't work for building materials or appliances. Sure, style and color are important, but it's just as easy to find a first-rate appliance that looks great in your new kitchen as it is to find one that looks fabulous but performs poorly. Keep function and quality as your primary criteria for selecting products.

LEFT
Handsome, enduring stone can be pricey. But it's the hottest trend in kitchen surfaces—and it's not going to cool down any time soon.

OPPOSITE
Ceramic tile, seen here on the floor, can look like natural stone, usually at less cost. To dress it up, the homeowners added a stone insert.

Step 5 PRORATE COSTS

You may be dismayed by the price of some items, but when you divide the cost of the product or material by its anticipated longevity (how many years you expect it to last), you may be amazed at how reasonable the price is. Of course, this won't alleviate an immediate cash-flow problem, but it will ease some of the sticker shock. An expensive product that will last for 20 years may be a better choice than a cheaper one that may have to be replaced in 5 years. Again, weigh that decision against how long you plan to stay in the house. Are the extra benefits worth spending the extra money?

Step 6 GUARANTEES AND SERVICE

Some offers are definitely better than others. Look at the warranty that comes from the manufacturer, as well as those offered by the place of purchase. A store may offer immediate replacement of the entire unit. While this may sound great, it isn't if you have to pay for labor or schedule time off from work for the removal and reinstallation of tile or a fixture. If all that is wrong with a faucet is a faulty washer, you may not want to yank out the entire unit. It should be your call. Find a place that offers a warranty based on the problems with the product. Ask about options in warranty coverage, and always get written copies of all warranties from the store or your contractor.

Step 7 DO A REALITY CHECK

Evaluate your situation, and choose the best products and materials for the way you live. Don't get swept away by bells and whistles that can blow your budget. A professional range with warming drawers and extra burners may appeal to your gourmet fantasy, but if your cooking routine consists of heating up last night's take-out food, invest the extra money elsewhere.

Step 8 LEAVE NOTHING TO CHANCE

Investigate every option and every detail. Don't find yourself bemoaning what you should have done once it's too late. After you have signed the final check is not the time to realize you could have installed a wall-mounted pot-filler faucet over your cooktop. Discover everything that's out there—before getting started and you won't have any regrets or extra charges for changes made after work has begun.

countertops

Selecting a countertop material is not as simple as it once was because there are infinitely more choices in color, pattern, and texture thanks to new materials and applications. The trend is to use more than one material, specifying types based on the functions at hand. For example, you might use a solid-surfacing material in one part of the kitchen, a marble insert at the bake center, and stainless steel next to the cooktop. Or you could pair one countertop material with the cabinetry that runs along the wall, and choose another for the island counter.

In addition to enhancing the function of your work surfaces, the countertop materials you choose can underpin your decorating theme. Wood is a natural choice for a country-style kitchen, for example, whereas concrete looks handsome in a contemporary setting. The concrete can be poured into a mold on site or prefabricated. You can add color to it or create a one-of-a-kind inlaid design with stones, shards of glass, china, tile, shells, or just about anything else you can think of.

There are no hard-and-fast rules about any material you choose, but one important factor that should play a role in your selection is maintenance. Some materials demand greater care than others. Marble, for

instance, must be sealed periodically because it can absorb liquids that will mar its looks. If you don't have time for the upkeep, can you live with the battle scars of everyday use?

Here's a rundown of your countertop material choices. After you've read about the attributes of each, you can decide which ones may be right for your application. Also, consider each type as a possibility for a matching or entirely different backsplash.

Plastic Laminate

There are probably more homes with plastic laminate kitchen counters than any other surface. Made of several layers of melamine, paper, and plastic resin bonded under heat and pressure, then glued to particleboard or plywood, it's inexpensive, relatively easy to install, and available in a vast array of

OPPOSITE
A natural wood floor adds undeniable warmth. If it's not in your price range, an affordable alternative is a laminate lookalike.

RIGHT
The natural markings in this granite are hard to duplicate, but some imitators come close to reproducing them.

colors and patterns. Plastic laminate resists stains, water, and mild abrasion very well, but it can be chipped or scratched by sharp knives, and it will scorch if you put a hot pot down on it. When it becomes seriously damaged, there is no repair option available except replacement.

More expensive color-through, or solid-core, laminates are similar to conventional laminate. However, because the color is solid all the way through, there are no unsightly black edges at the joints. Plus, you can layer and rout the edges of solid-core laminates to create decorative effects.

In addition to solid colors, there are laminates that offer the look of stone, leather, or wood, as well as patterns and visual textures. Small-scaled speckled patterns are popular today, and they easily camouflage minor scratches and spots. For the health-conscious, at least one manufacturer is offering a plastic laminate that features built-in antibacterial protection. The company claims that the treatment will not wash out and that it keeps bacteria, mold, and mildew from growing on your countertop. Colors are limited now, but look for more variety and some patterns in the near future.

Plastic laminate comes in various grades. Because it is generally affordable, don't skimp by purchasing the cheapest one you can find. To get your money's worth, select the highest quality, which won't chip easily and stays looking good longer. To keep it clean, use a mild detergent and damp sponge. Unless you seriously burn or scratch the surface, this countertop will last 10 to 15 years.

Solid-Surface Material

Solid color-through surfacing material is an extremely durable, easily maintained synthetic material made of polyester or acrylic. It's expensive, costing almost as much per linear foot as luxurious granite or marble, but it wears long and well. The material is completely impervious to water, and you can repair any dents or abrasions that may occur with a light sanding, but you should consult a professional installer to remove burns.

At first, solid-surfacing material was available only in shades of white or pastel colors, but now its palette has greatly expanded and includes faux-stone finishes. Because the color goes all the way through the thickness of the slab, it can be carved, inlaid, shaped, molded, even sandblasted to create a custom design.

Maintaining this countertop is easy using a mild non-abrasive cleanser and damp sponge. With a minimum amount of care, it will last 20 or more years.

Composite Material

Composite material is relatively new. Produced by binding stone chips (typically quartz) to powders and resins, it is an extremely hard and durable material that is becoming popular for countertops. Its textured and variegated look resembles stone, but the patterns formed are more consistent and the choice of colors is greater. Composite stone cleans easily and is heat and scratch-resistant. It doesn't need to be sealed or polished, either. Price-wise, it's almost comparable to natural stone.

Ceramic Tile

Ceramic tile is a perennial favorite. Impervious to water, it's perfect for installation at the sink. Tile is also durable, and it does not scratch, burn, or stain. Aside from its practical attributes, ceramic tile offers the greatest opportunity for adding color, pattern, and texture to your kitchen.

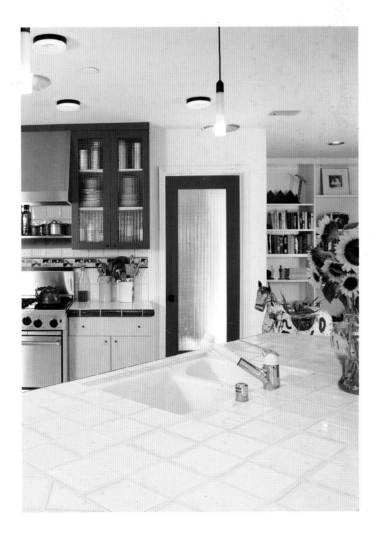

OPPOSITE
A solid-surface countertop can be enhanced in a number of decorative ways. Here, an inlaid strip of wood has been used as an edge treatment that matches the cabinet fronts.

LEFT
A waterfall edge treatment adds elegance to this solid-surface countertop.

RIGHT
The white ceramic-tile countertop around this kitchen sink looks pristine. But the grout must be sealed properly to inhibit the growth of bacteria.

smart tip

BACKSPLASHES

Because the space they occupy is relatively small, backsplashes offer the perfect opportunity to splurge on a luxurious material or an intricate design—or you can continue the countertop material for a unified look. Consider a custom mural behind the cooktop, for example. Try combining several tiles in different styles; create an interesting border. Check out glamorous glass and metal tiles, or simplify with painted bead board.

When shopping, you should also consider the finish. There are two kinds: unglazed and glazed. Unglazed tiles are not sealed and always come in a matte look. They are not practical for use near water unless you apply a sealant. On the other hand, glazed tiles are coated with a material that makes them impervious to water—or spills and stains from other liquids, too. This glaze on the tile can be matte or highly polished, depending on your taste.

You must regrout periodically. White grout shows dirt easily, but a dark-color one can camouflage stains. Still, unless it is sealed, grout will harbor bacteria. So clean the countertop regularly with a nonabrasive antibacterial cleanser. Tile that is well-maintained and regrouted when needed will last a lifetime.

For backsplashes and accents, don't overlook luminous glass tiles or metal tiles, which coordinate well with stainless-steel appliances and countertops.

OPPOSITE
Soapstone looks handsome paired with a medium-tone stained wood. This countertop material will hold up to heavy use and age to a soft charcoal gray.

LEFT
The speckles in granite make it particularly decorative. And it comes in various colors.

RIGHT
A concrete countertop, inlaid with small stones here, tiny pieces of metal, or bits of glass, can look elegant.

Stone

Granite is the most popular stone countertop material used in today's kitchens. Why do so many designers and homeowners like granite so much? First, it's handsome. An igneous rock, granite has a visible crystalline, coarse-grain texture. Its speckles and fine grains have been formed from quartz, feldspar, and mica, and bits of other materials that are present in the stone.

Granite comes in a variety of rich colors: shades of green, brown, gold, blue, violet, and mauve, as well as almost pure black and almost pure white. Another reason for its popularity is its endurance: granite is almost as hard as a diamond. Plus, it is practically non-porous. All of this means that it will last longer than your house and, unless it is exposed to some acidic liquids, like orange juice, for long periods of time, it doesn't stain. Dark colors will show fingerprints if the surface is highly polished. To keep it looking brand new, all you have to do is periodically seal it with a product that is available in any home center today. Then slice and dice on it, roll out dough on its cool surface, and simply wipe it with a damp cloth. Granite is expensive. However, instead of a slab, you can buy granite tiles, which are more affordable. Unlike a slab installation, granite tiling is a reasonably simple do-it-yourself project.

Another popular, elegant, and high-end material, marble is a soft, porous stone that can be gouged and stained easily. Even water leaves a mark. Still, it's a beautiful choice, and you will continue to appreciate it—even the little imperfections it may acquire over time—if you keep it properly sealed and treat it gently. Marble's cool surface makes it an excellent choice in a bake center or as a pullout slab that can be opened when needed. Just don't chop or slice food on it, and keep it clean. A marble countertop can serve you—and your kitchen—well for a lifetime.

Two other stone materials, limestone and concrete, are finding their way onto countertops in the hands of creative designers. Unlike the refined looks of granite and marble, these materials have a rustic, textured appeal. As with all natural materials, they are absorbent and must be sealed. Limestone is available as tiles, as is concrete, but the latter can be poured and molded, too. Becoming even more creative, designers are adding color to concrete. Some applications are carved or routed, even inlaid with tile or stone for an abstract look.

Wood

Wood is unrivaled for its natural warmth and beauty. Some cooks even love it when it starts to stain and scratch after lots of use. But wood also expands and contracts, depending on environmental conditions, and may warp if exposed to water, especially if it it not wiped up immmediately. To protect a wood countertop, apply a film finish of varnish or lacquer or oil it periodically. A film finish seals the wood, but it can crack and get water under it, which will cause peeling. You'll have to sand and reapply the coating every year. If you plan to chop or cut on it, treat the wood with nontoxic mineral oil, instead. Apply it every few months. When burns or stains occur, they can be sanded away.

Teak is an excellent selection for a wood countertop application. It's handsome and wears well. Another option is butcher block, which is actually a laminated wood product. Eastern hard rock sugar maple is the best for use in butcher block; it resists scratches, warping, and uneven wearing.

Stainless Steel

Many of today's kitchens feature lots of metal surfaces on appliances and counters. Stainless steel used for a countertop, whether it is for the entire counter or just a section of it, can look quite sophisticated, especially with a wood trim. What's practical about it is its capacity to take high heat without scorching, which makes it suitable as a landing strip for pots and pans straight from the cooktop. It is also impervious to water, so it's practical at the sink. On the negative side, stainless steel can be noisy to work on, and it will show smudges. Depending on the grade of the material, it may also be vulnerable to scrapes, stains, and corrosion. The higher the chromium and nickel content (and therefore the grade), the better. Also, look for a thick-gauge stainless steel that won't dent easily. A satin or brushed finish hides scratches. If you buy quality and care for it properly, a stainless-steel countertop should remain looking good and last at least 15 years.

OPPOSITE TOP
Butcher block is often selected for a small section of countertop or an island where it will be used primarily for chopping.

OPPOSITE BOTTOM
Stainless steel makes a lot of sense as countertop material next to the stove or cooktop because it can handle hot pots.

RIGHT
Wood and concrete surfaces pair beautifully in a modern kitchen.

flooring

As with every other product you select for the kitchen, flooring plays a role in establishing style, but it affects function, too. Generally, a material that is hard, such as stone or ceramic tile, can be uncomfortable to stand on for long periods of time. Resilient flooring and wood are more comfortable because they are more flexible than the others, having a bit of play in them. Therefore, consider your cooking style when you select a flooring material for the kitchen. If you prepare long, complex menus and are on your feet for extended periods of time, it may be wise to consider comfort over style.

Maintenance is another factor that should affect your decision about flooring. You'll have to weigh the different types, including their aesthetic and practical values, for yourself. Here's what you should know before you begin your comparison shopping.

Wood

The varieties of wood available as a flooring surface are vast, and the cost varies widely, depending on the type and grade of the wood and the choice of design—whether it will be strips or parquet. Some types work better than others for the kitchen.

Softwoods, such as pine and fir, are often used to make simple tongue-and-groove floor boards. Softwoods are usually less expensive than hardwoods, but they're also less durable and aren't suited for high-traffic areas, rooms with heavy furniture that can "dig" into the wood, or for surfaces in rooms where chairs or other furniture will be moved around frequently. The hardwoods—maple, birch, oak, or ash—are much less likely to mar with normal use, but hardwoods are far from indestructible; they will stand up to use, but not abuse, and you can't scrub them.

Color stains—reds, blues, and greens—may be appropriate in some kitchens, where a country or rustic feeling is desired. However, wood flooring is most often used to convey tone and feeling rather than a surface that brings color to a room. Natural wood stains range from the light ash tones to a deep coffee color. Generally, the lighter stains make a room feel more informal, and darker, richer stains suggest an atmosphere that is more traditional and reserved. Also, lighter stains—as with lighter paint or tile colors—create a feeling of openness and make a kitchen look larger, whereas darker stains tend to create an intimate feeling and reduce the visual expanse of a large space. The choice, however, is simply a personal one.

High-quality prefinished flooring, an increasingly popular alternative, eliminates the time, mess, and toxic fumes of the flooring-finishing process.

LEFT
Wood planks suit the rustic look of this kitchen. The light color of the wood stain, in contrast to the deep tone that is on the cabinets and the charcoal gray hue of the slate tiles, keeps the room bright.

OPPOSITE
Resilient vinyl floor tiles were used to create these earthy bands of color, in varied widths, in this contemporary kitchen. The colors and the softness underfoot counter the cool stainless-steel appliances.

The pattern of a wood floor also allows a designer to set the desired atmosphere of an interior. For example, for an Old World look, strips may be laid in a herringbone pattern. Decorative inlay with either strips or parquet patterns can enhance richness and visual interest and can be used to frame activity areas in large kitchens that have multiple activity zones. Hand-scraped wood appeals to those who like a rustic look.

As for maintenance, if a wood floor is properly sealed with polyurethane, its upkeep consists of vacuum-cleaning or dust-mopping as needed. It's important to promptly clean up any gritty material that may be tracked in from outdoors, because sand or gravel can scratch or even gouge the surface of a wood floor. If you take good care of your wood floor it should remain handsome for a lifetime.

Laminate Products

When your creative side says "wood" or "stone" but your practical side says "not a good idea in this room," the compromise may be laminate flooring, which is made from paper impregnated with melamine, an organic resin that is bonded to a core of particleboard, fiberboard, or other wood by-products. Laminate flooring can be installed over virtually any subflooring, including wood and concrete, as well as other surface flooring, such as ceramic or vinyl tiles, vinyl and other sheet flooring, and even certain types of carpeting. Also known as "faux wood" or "faux stone," depending on the finish, laminate may provide the look you desire along with the practical aspects you and your family can live with. Laminate is particularly well suited to kitchens, where stain and scratch resistance and quick cleanup are desirable. Manufacturers of this type of flooring offer warranties against staining, scratching, cracking, and peeling for up to 15 years. Laminate flooring cannot be refinished.

Vinyl and Other Resilient Flooring

Resilient flooring is available in sheet or tile form and is made from a variety of materials, including linoleum, asphalt or asphalt combined with asbestos, and rubber. However, the most commonly used material in manufacturing today's resilient flooring is vinyl plastic.

The most attractive features of resilient flooring include its price (making it among the most economical flooring options), its track record for long-lived, durable service, and its relatively easy maintenance. The variety of colors and patterns is vast, and as with tiles, the combinations of color and pattern are virtually limitless. You can find styles that resemble the look of more expensive flooring materials. Even the sheet form of resilient flooring can be customized with the use of inlay strips. You can design the pattern yourself or with help from a flooring specialist.

Cushioned sheet vinyl offers the most resilience. It has good stain resistance; it's comfortable and quiet underfoot; and many brands offer no-wax and never-wax finishes. All features are especially attractive if the floor in a kitchen gets lots of kid traffic. On the negative side, only the more expensive grades show an acceptable degree of resistance to nicking and denting, and although the range of available colors, patterns, and surface textures is great, sheet flooring isn't as flexible as vinyl tile when it comes to creating a customized look. On the plus side, sheet products are available in an array of patterns.

Regular sheet vinyl is less expensive than the cushioned types, but it carries the same disadvantages and is slightly less resilient. Except for the availability of no-wax finishes, a vinyl-tile floor is as stain resistant and as easy to maintain as sheet-vinyl products, but its resilience is fair at best. On the other hand, the design possibilities are greater with vinyl tiles because you mix and match them. You can expect a good-quality vinyl or resilient floor to last between 20 and 30 years.

BELOW
Ceramic tile is classic, and so is this black and white checker-board pattern. Small 2x2 tiles are perfect for the size of this space because larger tiles would overwhelm the room with such a bold pattern.

OPPOSITE
Italian stone tiles, cut into different sizes and shapes, have been installed in a complex arrangement here.

Ceramic Tile

Ceramic tile is an excellent choice for areas that are subjected to a lot of traffic and in rooms where resistance to moisture and stains is a factor. (Glass tile is not recommeded for floors.) These features—combined with the fact that maintenance involves a simple, soap-and-water cleaning—have made ceramic tile a handsome, centuries-old tradition for flooring. When shopping, look for tiles that are manufactured specifically for floor installation. Ones that are highly glazed, for example, are hazardous underfoot. Instead, choose soft-glazed versions. Ask the salesperson about the manufacturer's slip-resistance rating for the tile you are selecting, too. Unless the tile is handmade or imported, it's an affordable flooring choice that can last a lifetime. If you like but can't afford stone, you can find ceramic tiles that look remarkably like stone but cost less.

When you are creating a flooring design, consider whether the other elements in the room allow for an intricate pattern in the colors your creativity dictates. Or if you want to visually enlarge a small kitchen, choose one light color as the dominant feature in the pattern. Once that basic determination has been made, you can draw your design on a copy of your floor plan. You should also include a color sketch of the design on your sample board.

However, ceramic tile can be hard to live with: it's cold underfoot, noisy when someone walks across it in hard-soled shoes, and not at all resilient—expect the worst when something breakable falls on a tile floor.

Stone and Concrete

Along with ceramic tile, stone and concrete are among the flooring surfaces classified as "nonresilients." Like tile, properly sealed stone is unparalleled for durability, moisture- and stain-resistance, and ease of maintenance. It also shares with tile the drawbacks of being cold to the touch, noisy to walk on, and unforgivably hard—virtually guaranteeing that anything breakable that falls on a stone or concrete floor will not survive in one piece. The comparison with tile ends, however, with some critically important features. On the plus side is the fact that these floors are clearly, unmistakably natural. As good as some faux surfaces look (including some astonishingly good imitations, such as stone-look ceramic tiles), no product manufactured today actually matches the rustic irregularity of natural stone or the richness and depth of color in veined marble. The down side can be summed up in one word: cost. Whether it's slate, brick, concrete, limestone, sophisticated polished marble, or random-cut fieldstone, the material is expensive. However, it is durable and will last a lifetime. One caution: find out whether you'll need additional support under the floor to carry the weight of the material.

sinks, faucets, and more

Wh] at could be more basic to the modern kitchen than a sink and faucet? Yet in today's world, there's practically nothing basic about them. Style comes in all price ranges, but high-performance technology is accompanied by an equally high price tag. There are designs and finishes to suit any contemporary or traditional tastes. And far from being just necessary items in a kitchen, sinks and faucets have evolved into highly decorative elements, as well. Here's what's on the market.

Sinks

These receptacles come in all sizes, shapes, and colors, and are typically fabricated from enameled cast iron, stainless steel, a composite material (solid-surfacing, acrylic, or a mixture of natural quartz or granite with resins), or solid stone. They may be hand-painted or decorated with silk-screened designs, contoured, beveled, brushed to a matte finish, or polished to a mirror finish. The trend is to include the largest sink that you can accommodate within the confines of your space. Deep bowls make it easier to deal with awkward oversized items, such as large roasting pans and tall pots used for cooking pasta, and they help to cut down on splashing. A good example is the farm-style (or exposed-apron) sink that, at one time, would have been regarded as déclassé but is reemerging in glamorous solid colors or with decorative patterns. Shallow-basin sinks are available when there is no other place to install the dishwasher but under the sink.

Two- and three-bowl configurations are also gaining popularity. This arrangement allows you to separate clean dishes from dirty ones as well as from waste materials. Some sinks come with a colander and cutting board. A waste-disposal unit is typically installed with one of the bowls, usually the larger one. Just peel your potatoes, then whisk the skins down the drain. Lay the cutting board over the top of the bowl for chopping, and afterwards push the potato slices into the colander for rinsing. How's that for function?

Some designers recommend installing sinks in two separate areas. The primary sink often anchors the main food preparation and cleanup areas, while a smaller secondary sink serves outside of the major work zone. A second sink is a must when two or more people cook together routinely, but it is also handy if you practice crafts in the kitchen or entertain often and would use it as a wet bar. You can also use it as an extra place for washing hands when someone is using the main sink for preparing a meal.

Like every other kitchen product, there are numerous choices of sinks from which you will have to make a final selection, so it won't always be easy. In terms of durability, any one of the materials mentioned above will hold up well for years, if not decades, with the right care. Enameled cast-iron sinks tend to discolor but can be cleaned easily with a nonabrasive cleanser. Stainless steel and stone should be cleaned the same way. However, composite sinks are scratch resistant, with the exception of inexpensive acrylic models, so you can use an abrasive agent on them. Expect a quality sink to last as long as 30 years. In terms of installation, there are six types of sinks for the kitchen to consider.

■ **Undermounted.** If you want a smooth look, an undermounted sink may be for you. The bowl is attached underneath the countertop.

■ **Integral.** As the word "integral" implies, the sink and countertop are fabricated from the same material. There are no visible seams or joints in which food or debris can accumulate.

■ **Exposed apron.** Also called a "farmhouse sink," it is actually an undermount that reveals the sink's front panel.

■ **Self-rimming or drop-in.** A self-rimmed sink has a rolled edge that is mounted over the countertop.

■ **Rimmed**. Unlike a self-rimming sink, this type requires a flat metal strip to seal the sink to the countertop.

■ **Tiled-in.** Used with a tiled countertop, the sink rim is flush with the tiled surface. Grout seals the sink to the surrounding countertop area.

LEFT
This professional unit has a large sink with a built-in cooking vessel that boils, simmers, poaches, and steams foods.

BELOW
A small drop-in sink in the island creates a secondary work zone and can serve as a bar when company comes.

BOTTOM
An integral sink was fused with the countertop to make it look as if it came from one slab of solid-surfacing material.

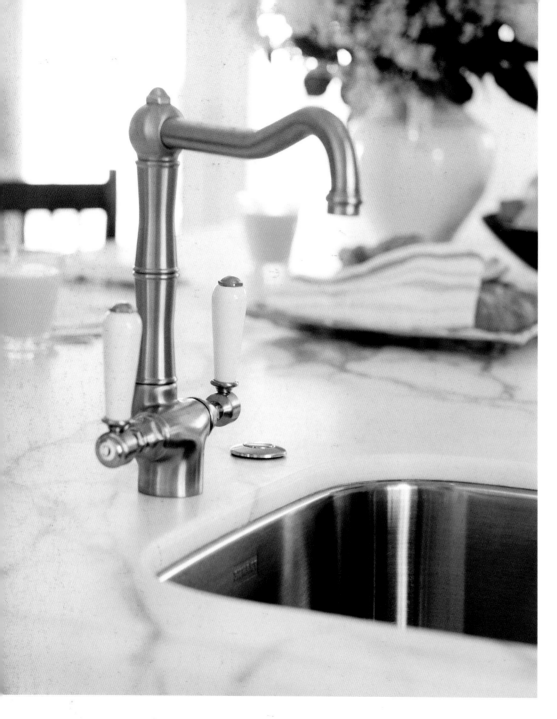

plumbing if you decide to install one of these faucets over your range or cooktop. The closer the cooktop or range is to the sink, the less expensive the job will be.

State-of-the-art technology in faucets gives you more control over water use and better finishes. Features to look for include pullout faucet heads, retractable sprayers, single-lever control, antiscald and flow-control devices, a lowered lead content in brass components, and built-in water purifiers to enhance taste.

For a quality faucet, inquire about its parts when you shop. The best are those made of solid brass or a brass-base material. Both are corrosion-resistant. Avoid plastic components—they won't hold up. Ask about the faucet's valving, too. Ball valves are good for single-lever faucets; ceramic-disk cartridges may be used in single- and dual-lever faucets. Try to buy a model that has washerless valving; it will cost more, but it will last longer and be less prone to leaks. This investment will save you money in the long run.

Besides selecting a spout type (standard, arched, gooseneck, or pullout), you may choose between single or double levers. Pullout faucets come with a built-in sprayer if you want one. Others require installing a separate sprayer. Until recently, a pressure-balanced faucet (one equipped with a device that equalizes the hot and cold water coming out of a faucet to prevent scalding), came only with single-lever models. Now this safety feature is available with faucets that have separate hot- and cold-water valves. You may mix your spout with one of many types of handle styles: wrist blades, levers, scrolls, numerous geometric shapes, and cross handles. If your fingers or hands get stiff, choose wrist blades, which are the easiest to manipulate.

Chrome, brass, enamel-coated or baked-on colors, pewter, and nickel are typical faucet finishes. Make a fashion statement

Faucets

Faucets are no longer just conduits for water. From sleek European-inspired designs to graceful gooseneck shapes, today's selections add beauty as well as function to a kitchen. An excellent example is the pot-filler faucet, which is mounted to the wall over the cooktop. Some versions have a pull-out spout; others come with a double- or triple-jointed arm that can be bent to reach up and down or swiveled back and forth, allowing the cook to pull the faucet all the way over to a pot on the farthest burner of a wide commercial range. Anyone who has ever had to lug a heavy pot of water from the tap to a burner will appreciate this convenience. Just remember: you'll need additional cold-water by mixing finishes or pair a matte, brushed, or antiqued look with one that is highly polished. Some finishes, such as chrome, are easier to care for than others; brass, for example, may require polishing. Always inquire about upkeep when you shop. Technologically advanced coatings can make even delicate finishes, like the enameled colors, more durable unless you use abrasive cleaners on them, which will scratch the finish. You may expect a good-quality faucet to last approximately 15 years; top-of-the-line products will hold up even longer.

In terms of installation, these are the three types of faucets from which to choose:

■ **Center set.** A center-set faucet features two separate valves, one for hot, the other for cold water, and a spout. However, all three pieces appear connected in one unit when they are installed.

smart tip

FANCY FAUCET FACTS

Chic faucet styling is not necessarily expensive. You can buy a good-looking kitchen faucet for less than a hundred dollars. But if you want high quality and more options you'll have to spend at least two or three times that much. For special finishes and features, expect the price to rise to about $1,000.

OPPOSITE
A center-set gooseneck faucet serves beautifully on this marble-topped island. Its elegant satin nickel finish is complemented by white porcelain handles.

RIGHT
This widespread installation is perfectly suited to a double-bowl sink. With lever-style handles, the taps are easily operated.

■ **Widespread.** Featuring a spout with two separate valves, a widespread faucet appears to be three distinct pieces.

■ **Single lever.** A single-lever installation contains a spout and solitary lever in one piece for one-hand operation.

When you design your sink and faucet area, don't be sidetracked by the good looks of a product. Think about whether it works for your application. Today, good looks come in all types. Instead, compare the size of your biggest pots and racks to see whether the sink you're considering will accommodate them. If it won't and you can't install something deeper, pair the sink with a pullout or gooseneck faucet. Always make sure it directs the flow of the water into the center of the bowl and slightly to one side. A spout that is proportionally too tall for the depth of the sink will splash water; one that is too short won't allow water to reach to the sink's corners. If you plan a double- or triple-bowl configuration, the spout should be long enough to deliver water to each of the separate bowls.

More conveniences

While you're at it, you might consider installing a waste-disposal unit. It's a convenient way to get rid of scraps, especially considering many localities have to separate food from debris for recycling. New disposal units don't make the awful noise that older models do, so they're more pleasant to operate. To keep the unit smelling fresh, drop a lemon wedge down into it occasionally. Check with your building inspector before installing a disposal unit, however. Depending on where you live, it may be either mandated or outlawed by code. The lifespan of a waste-disposal unit is 10 years.

Some faucets come with a built-in water filter in the spout. Water filtering is a good idea in the kitchen because it can protect against harmful chemicals, odor, dirt, rust, and more.

Another convenience you may want to include with your new sink and faucet is a hot- and cold-water dispenser. You can buy a unit that dispenses both, or just hot or cold water. They operate via a small lever or push button. Some brands are part of a water-filtration system.

LEFT
This restaurant-style faucet has an extra-long pull-down hose that maximizes the sprayhead reach. A highly functional design, it is particularly handy for wide or mutiple-bowl sinks.

OPPOSITE
In addition to a single-lever faucet with a pullout sprayer, this kitchen benefits from a built-in hot water on demand tap.

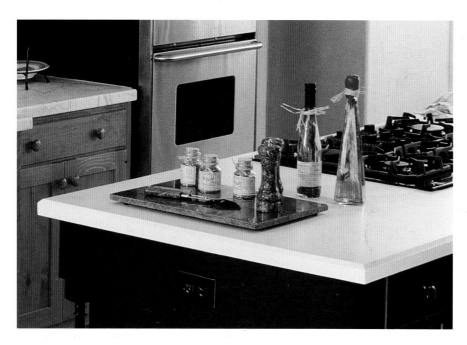

design workbook
CREATIVE COUNTERTOP THINKING

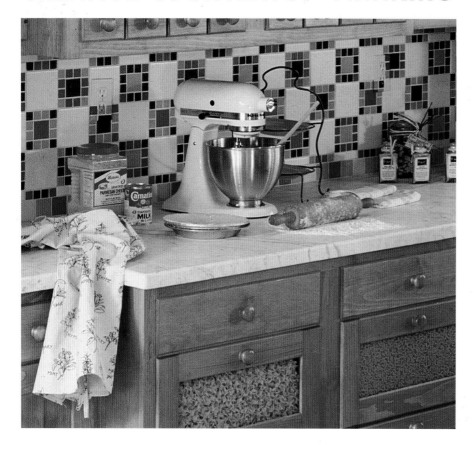

this surface is solid

At the cooktop, solid-surfacing material proves practical. It resists scratches, burns, and staining from acidic foods. (See also top left.)

stone is cool

For an ideal surface that will not stick when you roll dough on it, install a marble countertop (left). In a baking or pasta-making center, it's cool.

wood works

Butcher block (right) is an excellent surface for cutting vegetables and fruit. Near the sink, it has to be sealed against moisture and maintained regularly.

expand the space

By continuing the same type of flooring into areas that are adjacent to the kitchen, you will visually enlarge the impression of space.

play up pattern

Varying tones and natural patterns in wood planks add texture and interest to a floor. You can mix tile colors (top left) for a decorative effect, too.

design workbook
FLOOR THEM WITH GREAT STYLE

provide a platform

A dark floor (left) looks elegant. It's the perfect choice here, allowing formal-looking, white-painted wood cabinetry to stand out dramatically.

walk on the wild side

The natural colors, patterns, and textures used to give this kitchen (far left) its call-of-the-wild style are underscored by the unusual colored-concrete floor.

design workbook

KITCHEN SINK STRATEGY

central casting

A good-size sink in the main work zone is imperative. Here it's just steps away from the range and prep island.

supporting role

A second sink, in the island, left, is where produce can be rinsed before it is sliced and served or used for cooking.

identical twins

A pair of extra-deep farm sinks (bottom right) offer separate bowls for rinsing foods and washing dishes.

above all else

Style-wise, this sink (middle left) is outstanding. Mounted on the countertop, it offers an extra-deep bowl.

divide and conquer

This configuration (bottom left) divides a large sink into two compartments—main and secondary.

cabinetry and storage

CABINET CONSTRUCTION   CABINETS AS DECORATION   PLANNING STORAGE

an you relate to this? it's dinner time, and you need to pre-heat the oven. But wait. Did you take out the roasting pan, lasagna dish, muffin tins, and cookie sheets that are stored in there? Now where will you put them, with the counters covered with dinner ingredients?

The oven may have become the catchall for the big stuff that you can't fit into the cabinets. And the countertop may be cluttered with small appliances, canisters, your vitamins, or anything else. Cabinetry outfitted with organizing options can make your kitchen more efficient and a lot neater while establishing the decorative style of the room. This chapter

Learn about cabinet construction, finishes, hardware, and interior options before you choose this important part of your new kitchen.

teaches you what to look for in cabinets. Keep in mind, however, that cabinetry will also consume about 40 percent of your remodeling budget, according to the National Kitchen and Bath Association (NKBA).

cabinet construction

The quality of construction is a factor that always should be taken into consideration. How do you judge it? Solid wood is too expensive for most of today's budgets, but it might be used on just the doors and frames. More typical is plywood box construction, which offers good structural support, and solid wood on the doors and frames. To save money, cabinetmakers sometimes use strong plywood for support elements like the box and frame, and medium-density fiberboard for other parts like doors and drawer fronts. In yet another alternative, good-quality laminate cabinets can be made with high-quality, thick particleboard underneath the laminate finish. The material will hold screws securely, and the cabinet won't warp over time.

There are other things to look for in cabinet construction. They include dovetail or mortise-and-tenon joinery and solidly mortised hinges. Also, make sure the interior of every cabinet is well finished, with adjustable shelves that are a minimum ⅝-inch thick to prevent bowing.

Manufacturing Styles

Unless you have the time and skill to build the cabinets yourself or can hire someone else to do it, you'll have to purchase them in one of four ways: knockdown (also known as RTA, or ready to assemble), stock, semi-custom, or custom. Prices vary from category to category, and even within each category. To make the wisest choice, be sure you know the differences that distinguish one type from another.

■ **Custom cabinets** are not limited in terms of style or size, because they are built to the designer's specifications. They are made from scratch, sometimes on-site or at the manufacturer, so they can take up to three months to be completed. The wait is worth it: these cabinets look like fine furniture in both their detailing and color. Of course, such craftsmanship isn't cheap. Custom cabinets can run in price from moderate to extremely expensive.

■ **Semi-custom cabinets,** like custom ones, are made to measure, but by a large cabinet company at a price that is usually considerably lower than a local millwork shop would charge. This means they take about eight weeks to be delivered. As with all things, the cost will ultimately depend on quality, finish, and any extra features you order. Although styles and shapes are standard, semi-custom cabinets are produced to fit the homeowner's specific needs, which may include special sizes, interior organizers, and custom finishes.

■ **Stock cabinets** are often available on the spot where they are sold or can be delivered quickly. Although they come in a great variety of standard sizes, making it easy for you to find what you need, they are limited in style and color. This means you can mix and match stock cabinets for a custom look, but you won't find a great selection from which to choose. However, you will find more interior features that only came with custom or semi-custom models not so long ago.

The quality of stock cabinets varies greatly by manufacturer and ranges from slightly below adequate to excellent. Inquire about what materials were used in the manufacture, the grade (quality) of the materials, and the type of joinery. Don't buy anything that is simply glued together—unless you plan to sell the house soon and just want to update the appearance of the kitchen to attract buyers.

smart tip CABINET DOOR STYLE CHOICES

Door styles are strictly decorative. Styles pictured, left to right: reveal-overlay panel; frame and panel; flat panel; beaded frame and panel; square raised panel; curved raised panel; bead-board panel; and cathedral panel

smart tip CABINETS: FRAMED VERSUS FRAMELESS

FRAMED cabinets have a traditional look, with a full frame across the face of the cabinet box that may show between closed doors. This secures adjacent cabinets and strengthens wider cabinet boxes with a center rail. Hinges on framed cabinets may or may not be visible. The door's face may be ornamented with raised or recessed panels, trimmed or framed panels, or a framed-glass panel.

FRAMELESS cabinets—also known as European-style cabinets, although American manufacturers also make them—are built without a face frame and sport a clean, contemporary look. There's no trim or molding with this simple design. Close-fitting doors cover the entire front of the box, no ornamentation appears on the face of the doors, and hinges are typically hidden inside the cabinet box.

■ **Knockdown cabinets** are the most economical choice. They are basically stock cabinets that are shipped flat, and sometimes arrive unfinished. The cost savings are realized because you put the pieces together yourself, and possibly you stain or paint and then install the cabinets yourself, too. The variety of styles is limited but current, and you can add personality with a special finish and interesting hardware. You don't have to be particularly handy to put together knockdown cabinets. Most require using a screwdriver and wrench. But you do have to invest the time in their assembly. This is a sensible choice if you are on a tight budget or you don't want to invest too much money in a kitchen renovation.

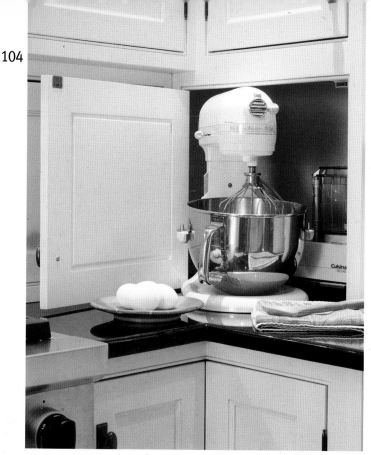

Cabinet Accessories and Options

Most people would agree that no matter how much storage space they have, they need even more. The problem often isn't the amount, it's the inaccessible placement and inefficient configuration of the storage space. One of the greatest benefits today's designers and manufacturers offer is fitted and accessorized interiors that maximize even the smallest nook and cranny inside cabinets and drawers. These accommodations not only expand the use of space but increase convenience and accessibility. Among them are:

■ **Appliance Garages**. Appliance garages make use of dead space in a corner, but they can be installed anywhere in the vertical space between wall-mounted cabinets and the countertop. A tambour (rolltop) door hides small appliances like a food processor or anything else you want within reach but hidden from view. This form of mini-cabinet can be equipped with an electrical outlet and can even be divided into separate sections to store more than one item. Reserve part of the appliance garage for cookbook storage, or outfit it with small drawers for little items or spices. Customize an appliance garage any way you like. Include lighting, too.

■ **Built-in Pantry Units.** These fold-out or slide-out units can be fitted into narrow areas that might otherwise remain wasted. Store dry or canned goods here.

■ **Lazy Susans and Carousel Shelves.** These rotating shelves maximize dead corner storage and put items like dishes or pots and pans within easy reach. A Lazy Susan rotates 360 degrees, so just spin it to find what you're looking for. Carousel shelves, which attach to two right-angled doors, rotate 270 degrees; open the doors and the shelves, which are actually attached to the doors, put any item within hand reach. Pivoting shelves are a variation on the carousel design and may or may not be door-mounted. In addition, units may be built into taller cabinets, creating a pantry that can store a lot in a small amount of space.

■ **Fold-Down Mixer Shelf.** This spring-loaded shelf swings up and out of a base cabinet for use, then folds down and back into the cabinet when the mixer is no longer needed.

■ **Slide-Outs and Tilt-Outs.** Installed in base cabinets, slide-out trays and racks store small appliances, linens, cans, or boxed items, while slide-out bins are good for holding onions, grains, pet food, or potting soil—even garbage or recycling containers. A tilt-out tray is located in the often-wasted area just below the lip of the countertop in front of the sink and above base cabinet doors. It looks like a drawer but tilts open to provide a nook for sponges and scouring pads that tend to look messy when left on the counter.

In addition to these options, check out everything a manufacturer has to offer to make the most of a cabinet's storage capacity. Other items to look for include special racks for trays and cookie sheets; drawer inserts for organizing spices and utensils; watertight recycling bins; wine racks; fold-down recipe book rests; sliding pot racks; built-in canister drawers; and plate racks.

cabinets as decoration

The look you create in your kitchen will be largely influenced by the cabinetry you select. Finding a style that suits you and how you will use your new kitchen is similar to shopping for furniture. In fact, don't be surprised to see many fine furniture details dressing up the cabinets on view in showrooms and home centers today.

Besides architectural elements like fluted pilasters, corbels, moldings, and bull's-eye panels, look for details like fretwork, rope motifs, gingerbread trim, balusters, composition ornamentation (which looks like carving), even footed cabinets that mimic separate furniture pieces. If your taste runs toward less fussy design, you'll also find handsome door and drawer styles that feature minimal decoration, if any.

Woods and finishes are just as varied, and range from informal looks in birch, oak, ash, and maple to rich mahogany and cherry. Laminate finishes, though less popular than they were a decade ago, haven't completely disappeared from the marketplace, but color has been added to the once-ubiquitous palette of almond and white finishes.

Color is coming on strong on wood cabinetry, too. Accents in one, two, or more hues are pairing with natural wood tones. White-painted cabinets take on a warmer glow with tinted shades of this always popular neutral. Special "vintage" finishes, such as translucent color glazes, continue to grow in popularity, as do distressed finishing techniques such as wire brushing and rubbed-through color that add both another dimension and the appeal of handcraftmanship, even on mass-produced items. Contemporary kitchens, which historically favor an all-white palette, are warming up with earthier neutral shades, less sterile off-whites, and even color.

If you're shy about using color on such a high-ticket item as cabinetry, try it as an accent on molding, door trim, or on the island cabinetry. Just as matched furniture suites have become passé in other rooms of the house, the same is true for the kitchen, where mixing motifs or creating an unfitted look can add sophistication and visual interest.

Designers use the warmth of wood and the personality of

LEFT
It's possible to create a furniture-like server or hutch using cabinetry components. Glass doors keep the contents on view but cleaner than if stored on open shelves.

OPPOSITE TOP LEFT
Choose cabinets in several different finishes to create an interesting unfitted look.

OPPOSITE TOP RIGHT
Most cabinet manufacturers offer a complete line of trim pieces so that you can detail your new kitchen with moldings, pilasters, corbels, and medallions if that suits your tastes.

OPPOSITE BOTTOM
Clean, uncluttered lines and a high-gloss finish are hallmarks of the contemporary look for cabinetry. Keep accessories to a minimum, and choose stainless-steel and glass accents if you want your new kitchen to have contemporary flair.

color to balance the high-tech look of commercial-style equipment. Homeowners want their kitchens to work harder, but they don't want them to look industrial. Rather than appearing incongruous, this blending of traditional and commercial materials is surprisingly appealing.

Hardware

Another way to emphasize your kitchen's decorative style is with hardware. From exquisite reproductions in brass, pewter, wrought iron, or ceramic to handsome bronze, chrome, nickel, glass, steel, plastic, rubber, wood, or stone creations, a smorgasbord of shapes and designs is available. Some pieces are highly polished; others are matte-finished, smooth, or hammered. Some are abstract or geometrical; others are simple, elegant shapes. Whimsical designs take on the forms of animals or teapots, veg-

etables or flowers. Even just one or two great-looking door or drawer pulls can punch up a kitchen that may be lacking personality. Like mixing cabinet finishes, a combination of two hardware styles—perhaps picked up from other materials in the room—makes a big design statement. Fortunately, there is a large variety of stock styles and finishes from which to choose. Many styles look high-end but are affordable. Many cabinet manufacturers offer hardware when you purchase cabinets. See what the stock offerings are. If none of these appeals to you, shop at an independent retailer for hardware that may suit your style more closely.

Besides looks, consider the function of a pull or knob. You have to be able to grip it easily and comfortably. If your fingers or hands get stiff easily or if you have arthritis, select C- or U-shaped pulls. If you like a knob, try it out in the showroom to make sure it isn't slippery or awkward when you grab it. Knobs and pulls can be inexpensive if you can stick to unfinished ones that you can paint in an accent color. If you don't plan to buy new cabinets, changing the hardware on old ones can redefine their style.

planning your storage

ow that you know that there are cabinets and accessories that make the most disorganized person's kitchen a model of neatness and efficiency, a thoughtful approach to planning storage for the new design is in order. The time to do this is before plans are on paper or work has begun. Here are a few ideas to get you started.

smart steps
suit your lifestyle

■ **Step 1** ANALYZE YOUR NEEDS

Make a detailed list of your shopping and cooking habits. How do you buy food? If you buy in bulk, how much of it has to be stored in the refrigerator? Do you need special storage for wines or bottled vinegars? A lot of canned goods, boxed grains, and pasta will need cabinet space. The National Kitchen and Bath Association (NKBA) conducted a study several years ago that revealed that most kitchens regularly store 18 cans of vegetables, 23 spices, and six boxes of cereal. How does yours compare?

Think about your cooking and serving utensils. Where are you most likely to use them? In the preparation area? By the cooktop? In both places? If you frequently use a wok or other typically awkward items, you might want to design special compartments or open shelves that keep them handy but hidden when not in use. The NKBA study says that most kitchens house 791 pots, pans, and dishes. (That includes glassware and china.) Are most of your utensils presently contained in the kitchen? Would you like to add the storage to do so?

Are your smaller appliances, such as a mixer and food processor, handheld or larger? Are they heavy or awkward to move? If so, including an appliance garage on your counter in your design makes sense if you use these items often.

Somehow the kitchen is the catchall for many non-cooking- and noneating-related items, too. If you don't think that will change once your new kitchen is completed, prepare for it. If, for example, your craft supplies, gardening tools, outdoor grilling items, and cleaning supplies are now stored on the countertop or on top of the refrigerator, reserve space for them on your formal plan—either inside a cabinet, in the pantry, or on shelves.

■ **Step 2** COMPARTMENTALIZE

It makes great organizational sense to store like items together. Make a plan now to store similar items, such as all baking pans on one shelf, all cookbooks in one

spot. Plan to store cooking utensils in one or two drawers near prep areas and to keep all the pots and pans
together. Shelve foods by type, so that you keep all
the cereals in one area, all the snack foods in another,
and all beverages together. Plan now to tailor your
shelf heights to meet these needs. Not only will this
maximize the use of space, it will make finding what
you need quicker and easier.

Step 3 INSTALL CABINET ACCESSORIES

The specialized storage options detailed earlier can be
a little pricey, but they are less expensive if you purchase them with your cabinetry. Adding them later or
retrofitting them into older cabinetry can boost the cost
even higher. If funds are restricted, perhaps you could
limit them to a few.

There are other accessories that can keep items
neatly organized when cabinet space is at a premium.
Besides the ubiquitous wire shelf and bin options, a
wall- or ceiling-mounted pot rack can make use of otherwise overlooked overhead space. A knife rack that
attaches to the wall or the outside of a cabinet is also
handy. Wall racks that hold wine, barware, spices,
mops and brooms, and ironing boards are negligible in
price, but invaluable space savers.

Step 4 PLAN TO RECYCLE

Don't make recycling an afterthought. If you don't want
to run outdoors to the various recycling receptacles, try
to incorporate a place in the kitchen to separate them
unobtrusively. Slide-out bins are an excellent solution if
you can spare the cabinet space. In some kitchens a
slide-out can accommodate two containers: the one in
front is reserved for nonrecyclables; the second container is solely for recyclable trash.

Step 5 BE HONEST ABOUT YOUR HABITS

If you're not a particularly neat person, avoid open
shelving. The same advice applies to glass-fronted cabinets. Use just one or two of these cabinets for an
attractive display.

Now that you have analyzed both your kitchen
lifestyle and cooking style, you're ready to move on.
The honest evaluation of your wants, needs, and preferences has prepared you to deal with the next big
question—what about appliances?

LEFT
Clear glass doors offer an unhindered view of cabinet contents but also require a disciplined approach to storage in order to stay attractive.

ABOVE
Plan to keep only items that are used frequently, and thus cleaned often, on open shelves and hooks.

BELOW
Make recycling easy by including the appropriate containers.

design workbook

CABINETS FILL MANY NEEDS

unite separate spaces

Blend an open-plan kitchen with an adjoining room by selecting cabinetry with a furniture-like finish and detailing for both spaces.

provide flexibility

Include a wide variety of storage options, including tall units, narrow and deep drawers, and both solid and glass doors. (See also top left.)

set a decorative tone

It's possible to personalize your new kitchen with cabinets made from exotic woods and finished with a custom-mixed color, far left.

conceal appliances

Most cabinet manufacturers offer a wide range of options designed to seamlessly integrate appliances so that they all but disappear or can be built-in. (See also left.)

design workbook
DIVIDE AND CONQUER CLUTTER

use all the space

Extend the cabinets all the way to ceiling height to gain storage space for infrequently used items, such as holiday cookie cutters and tins.

custom-made to fit

A drawer insert, top left, that's custom-made to hold every gadget you own could help to maintain a serene and orderly kitchen.

a spot for everything

It's easy to maintain order when every item has a home. Even kids can help put utensils away in a compartmentalized drawer, far left.

build in safety

Many cabinet manufacturers offer drawer inserts, left, that not only protect knife blades by separating them but also keep hands that reach inside the drawer safe from cuts.

6

choosing appliances

RANGES   COOKTOPS AND OVENS   REFRIGERATORS AND FREEZERS
NEAR-THE-SINK APPLIANCES   SHOPPING TIPS

Today's appliances are status symbols, and the vast selection of models and features is dazzling. With such a variety, it's important to analyze your needs carefully before you shop. New appliances will consume a considerable portion of your remodeling budget, so you've got to choose wisely. Most major kitchen appliances will last as long as 15 to 20 years. The way to get the most for your money is to purchase the model and size that's right for your lifestyle now—and for the not-too-distant future. When you shop, always remember: the equipment you own should not determine what's for dinner. Rather, whoever does the cooking should decide what kind of equipment he or she requires. Thankfully, today you can custom-equip a kitchen with the types of appliances that cater to the tastes and habits of both cook and family.

Today's residential kitchen appliances can provide average consumers with as many professional cooking features as possible.

ranges, cooktops, and ovens

There are two basic questions you'll have to answer up front about your cooking equipment. What kind of fuel does it use, gas or electric, and will it be a configuration of separate cooktop and oven units or will it be contained in one unit? In today's world, you can combine fuels in the same appliance or separately.

If you can't make up your mind about fuel, you should at least know that the type you select makes a difference. After reviewing the advantages and disadvantages of each, you may want to combine both types into your plans.

Should you install a range or a separate cooktop and oven or ovens? The range is a smart choice if you have limited space. It may also be the most economical option because you won't incur the cost of multiple hookups and additional ventilation. However, it's not the best choice when more than one cook will work in the kitchen at the same time. And let's face it, when you're stirring the pot on top of the stove while roasting something in the oven, the heat buildup can become uncomfortable if not unbearable.

Ranges

You generally have a choice between a freestanding range, a slide-in model that fits between two base cabinets and sits on the floor, or a drop-in version, which is installed between two cabinets and must be fastened to the side of each of them. A drop-in range needs a base, which is normally constructed of wood. Drop-ins can hang from the countertop or sit on a low cabinet base. They are usually installed with a matching cabinet panel under them to provide storage. Drop-ins offer an economical approach to a built-in custom look, with minimal space required. Both the slide-in and drop-in models are designed to look built-in: the controls are placed in front of the unit so they can be used in islands or peninsulas as well as in a straight run of wall cabinetry.

If you are replacing your old range with a new one that has to fit into a preexisting opening, measure the front of the old unit. The typical size is 30 inches wide, although you can find both narrower and wider models. Extras to look for include interchangeable modular elements such as a drop-in wok, a grill or griddle, sealed burners, high- and low-heat burners, continuous grills, a warming drawer, and a self-cleaning oven.

Separate cooktops and ovens

Separate cooktops and wall ovens are convenient if you have the room. This arrangement allows you to customize the work centers and install them where they fit best into the traffic pattern and work flow. It is ideal in a kitchen with multiple cooks. Modular units let you tailor your cooking system to the way you cook. Besides two-, four-, five-, six-, or eight-burner units, you can purchase accessories—built-in units or detachable, interchangeable parts for greater flexibility and easy cleanup. If you can afford the cost of adding extra ventilation and want to create even more convenience for two cooks, install four or six burners in one part of the work area and an additional pair elsewhere, such as a snack zone.

Another practical device is a warming drawer; models made for the residential market are built-in. You can purchase a commercial unit, which can be freestanding or built-in, but it carries a higher price tag. Either version measures 24 or 27 inches. Most manufacturers make warming drawers to match other appliances in their lines, but you can outfit them with a trim finish that blends with the cabinetry, as well. Look for a model with an adjustable setting that ranges from crisp to moist and comes with flexible racks.

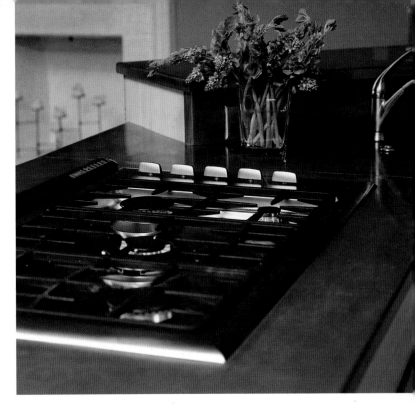

OPPOSITE

A range can provide a combination of fuels. Most gourmet cooks prefer gas burners and electric or convection ovens.

ABOVE

Working at the stove while something is roasting in the oven can be uncomfortable—a good case for separate appliances.

BELOW

A warming drawer near the oven makes it easy to keep baked or roasted items warm before serving.

Gas Cooking Appliances

The bottom line is: you need heat—and lots of it. But you must to be able to control it and adjust it easily and quickly. In that department, gas delivers, which is why professional chefs prefer it. For better, quicker cooking results, burners have to produce at least 15,000 Btu (British thermal units, the measurement for heat output), but gas burners manufactured for the residential market typically deliver 30 to 50 percent less than that amount. That's why you can never prepare a steak at home that tastes quite as good as one that has been prepared in a restaurant. You can't raise the flame high enough to sear the meat properly.

Should you buy a commercial range? Probably not. The tremendous heat it generates will increase the risk of fire and injury in your home. Codes for installing this type of range are strict—some areas even prohibit the installation of commercial equipment. A commercial range also requires special venting and minimum clearances between it and adjacent cabinets or combustible materials or surfaces. However, you may want to consider a commercial-style range, which will allow you to set flames as high as 18,000 Btu and to bring them down to 360 Btu (on some models) for low simmering. In fact, for a slightly higher price, many models come with the option of one high-flame burner (12,000 to 18,000 Btu) and one low-simmer burner in addition to regular burners and a larger-than-standard capacity oven.

If you think gas cooktops are difficult to keep clean, sealed gas burners may be the answer because the cooking surface is extended around the heating element. No more drip plates and no more escaping flames. In addition, some gas cooktops come equipped with electronic ignition; some models will automatically reignite if a pot boils over and extinguishes the flame—that's a smart safety feature.

You can adjust the flame, use any size pot, and cook more evenly on a gas burner. If you want to switch from electric to gas service, you'll need to run a gas line into the kitchen besides buying the new appliance. First check with the building department in your area, and then speak to a plumber who can install and route the pipe. The price of the job depends on the complexity of your situation. A free estimate is always worth the time it takes.

For the look and charm of an old-fashioned cast-iron stove, you might consider an English import, the AGA cooker, which uses natural gas or propane to create the radiant heat of a wood- or coal-burning type. (Authentic wood- or coal-burning models are also available.) This is an heirloom-quality appliance

OPPOSITE

Professional cooks and weekend gourmets alike prefer gas-fueled cooktops or ranges like this one because the high- and low-flame burners allow for proper searing and precise simmering.

RIGHT

The burners on this gas cooktop can be adjusted conveniently to output as low as 500 Btu or as high as 18,000 Btu.

design workbook

DESIGN YOUR OWN COOKTOP

integrated cooktop

This dual-fuel cooking station features a high-output gas burner, a steamer, and an electric cooktop.

mini hub

A compact secondary cooking zone, top left, may combine a two-burner electric cooktop with a steamer.

fire station

For steak and French fry lovers, a built-in grill and deep fryer can complement gas burners, center left.

wok master

This 18,000 Btu burner, bottom far left, is dedicated to wok cooking, which requires extremely high heat.

flapjacks and more

A steel griddle, left, is another option that is available on some high-end cooktops and ranges.

with a cooktop that features a warming plate, boiling plate, and simmering plate. Insulating lids cover the latter elements when they are not in use. Some models have four ovens for baking, roasting, warming, and simmering, but a two-oven cooker is also available. The AGA can be vented through a flue to the outdoors; a down-draft type of vent is also available and allows placement of the cooker anywhere in the room.

If this appeals to you, you should know that the conventional AGA cooker has to stay on all the time because it takes hours to heat up, but it is energy efficient. Still, if you live in a warm climate or don't have air conditioning, you may find that it makes the kitchen stuffy. There is a new model that features standard gas burners and two electric ovens. An AGA cooker usually costs about ten times more than what you'll pay for a standard gas range—so check your bottom line before planning your design around it.

For Francophiles, the French La Cornue stove has similar visual appeal and a bit more technology. Some newer models feature a combination of high- to low-heat gas and electric burners for cooking and baking versatility.

Electric Cooktops

Despite the virtues of gas fuel, some people feel more comfortable with electric burners because they don't like the idea of an exposed flame. If that's your preference, you should know that watts are to electric cooktops what Btu is to gas-powered models. The more wattage, the quicker-cooking the cooktop. There are several kinds to consider.

■ **Coil Elements.** The traditional electric cooking surface is the least expensive. Using conduction and radiation, coils heat up quickly but take time cooling, so you can't go from sizzle to simmer instantly as you can with gas. And although you can use a variety of cookware, pans must have flat bottoms and extend no more than 2 inches beyond the heating element for optimal results.

■ **Ceramic Glass.** Also called radiant-heat cooking surfaces, ceramic cooktops feature electric-resistance coils directly under translucent glass, which transfers heat more efficiently to the cookware than older, opaque, white ceramic surfaces. It also uses higher-wattage heating elements. The smooth, sleek appearance of ceramic glass cooktops appeals to contemporary tastes. The finish is scratch- and stain-resistant, but it can be damaged by abrasive cleansers. You'll need flat-bottomed, heavy-gauge metal pans to heat food quickly and effectively with ceramic glass, and cookware should not extend more than 1 inch beyond the cooking area.

■ **Halogen.** Similar to ceramic glass cooktops, especially with regard to cookware and cleaning, halogen units combine electric-resistance heating wires and halogen lamps that are located beneath a ceramic-glass cover to create heat.

■ **Induction.** Also featuring a ceramic-glass surface, induction-type cooking technology uses electromagnetic energy to heat the cookware, not the cooktop, making it safe because no heat is generated by a flame or coil. An induction cooktop is also easy to keep clean: because the surface remains relatively cool, the spills won't burn and turn into a crusty mess that requires bothersome scrubbing.

Below the surface, the coils produce a high-frequency alternating magnetic field that flows through the cookware. Most of the heat on the cooktop is transferred from the pan. Without a pan or utensil, the heating coil is de-energized and turns itself off. Induction cooktops require magnetic-responsive cookware, which means pots and pans for use with this appliance must be steel, porcelain-on-steel, stainless steel, or cast iron.

Manufacturers of induction cooktops boast of its quick response—it can go from high heat to low heat instantly—and precise temperature control.

OPPOSITE

An electric cooktop like this one, which uses induction technology, has a ceramic-glass surface that stays cool to the touch because only the cookware gets hot.

ABOVE

This freestanding electric range features a cooktop with a three-ring element that will accommodate various-size pans.

smart tip COMMERCIAL-STYLE RANGES

Don't assume that a commercial-style range is the same as a "professional-style" unit. Professional style usually means the appliance is finished in stainless steel so it looks like a commercial model. This is fine if you like the appearance of commercial equipment, and that's the only reason you're buying it. But if you want more power, choose commercial-style. To be on the safe side, ask the dealer or salesperson about the Btu level of the burners on the model before you buy it.

Ovens

An oven has to be well insulated to bake evenly and broil foods adequately. Again, fuel is an important factor. Many professional chefs prefer electric ovens because they brown food more uniformly than gas models. Broiling, however, is done best at a high temperature, which would tend to recommend gas. Designers often specify two ovens for layouts that can accommodate more than one work triangle. (See Chapter Two: "Designing a Smart Layout.") If two ovens can work in your plan, you could install one powered by gas for broiling while reserving the electric oven for baking. If you have only enough room for a range, you can buy a dual-fuel model—gas burners and an electric oven.

Size is another consideration. An oven with extra capacity will cost more, but it's definitely an advantage. Kitchen designers are increasingly recommending 27- and 30-inch models over the standard 24-inch versions. If you really need it, a 36-inch model is available. As a frame of reference when making up your mind regarding the size you need, remember: you can roast a 20-pound turkey nicely in a standard-size oven.

Wall ovens are the easiest and safest to use when they are installed at waist height. If you can afford a pair of ovens, don't install them one above the other; either the bottom one will require unneccessary awkward bending, or the top unit will be too high for safely transferring food. Ideally, two wall ovens should be placed side by side or located in two separate work areas.

For ease of maintenance, shop for a self-cleaning model. The cleaning systems of electric ovens are more effective than those of gas-powered units because of their even heat distribution. Also, poke your head into the cavity of any oven you're considering; dark interiors retain heat and hide grime better than light ones. Test the racks. Are they easy to maneuver yet secure in place? Is the light bulb accessible for changing it? Is it bright enough? Digital clocks and timers; preset options for baking, cleaning, timing, and temperature settings; and push-button temperature controls are some of the extra features you can have with a new oven—at an additional price.

■ **Convection Ovens.** You may want to consider a convection oven as a second oven, if only because it can't broil. (The heating source is located outside the cavity.) It works as follows: the oven circulates heated air around the food, pulls the air out of the cooking cavity, reheats the air over a hot element, and returns the reheated air to the cavity. It does have a drying effect,

expensive than standard models but perhaps not more than the cost of all three combined.

■ **Microwave Ovens.** Microwave units cut down cooking time for some foods to mere minutes, with more-powerful models (750 to 1,000 watts) cooking faster. But roasts don't brown, and meat, fish, and fowl must be covered for at least part of the cooking time to prevent overcooking. Microwave-oven cookware should be mostly nonmetallic—anything ceramic, most plastics, and paper—because dishes or pans with a metal coating or trim may cause arcing.

However, microwave ovens also have their advantages. They defrost and reheat foods quickly and efficiently, which is great for busy families. A model with an extra shelf lets you reheat more than one dish at a time, and ones equipped with sensors can tell when some foods are done by the amount of steam or humidity they produce during cooking. Temperature-sensitive devices can be preset to reduce heat from a cooking to a warming level once the food gets hot enough. Another program allows you to indicate the weight of the food item, then rely on the microwave to decide how long to cook it and the appropriate heat

so you don't want to cook foods in a convection oven that should retain lots of moisture, but it's terrific for baking pastry or roasting chicken because it makes outer layers crisp. Other advantages to a convection oven include its ability to bake or roast faster than a conventional model, at temperatures that are 25 to 75 degrees Fahrenheit lower, which saves energy. And because superheating the air over hot elements burns off odors, it's possible to bake dissimilar foods, such as pound cake and pizza, at the same time. There are some multiple-mode models on the market that can switch from conventional- to convection- to microwave-oven cooking, although they are considerably more

level. Installation on or under a shelf that's at eye level makes it easy to monitor microwave cooking, but a countertop installation is also acceptable. Place a microwave near the refrigerator if you'll use it often to prepare frozen food or reheat cold meals, or locate it in a secondary work zone so that the kids can make snacks without getting in your way. If it is at all possible, do not place a microwave on a high shelf or on top of the refrigerator. Remember: in addition to the type of cooking appliances and the cost of any optional features you purchase, factor in the potential price of replacing any or all of your cookware. Again, let your lifestyle and cooking style lead your way.

Ventilation

No discussion of cooking equipment is complete without addressing ventilation. The grease, smoke, heat, and steam generated when you cook will take their toll on your new cabinets, countertops, floors, walls, and other surfaces, where they collect along with germs and general grime. The only efficient way to combat this residue and the stale cooking odors that linger is with an exhaust system. A fan over the range or cooktop is not enough. The most effective way to ventilate a kitchen is with a hooded system. The hood, which is installed directly over the cooking surface, captures the bad air as it heats and naturally rises. A fan expels the contaminants to the outside through a duct. A damper inside the hood closes when the system is turned off so that cold air can't enter the house from the outside. Don't try to save money by installing a ductless fan: any system that isn't ducted to the outside is useless.

Although handsome hoods can create a focal point in the kitchen, most people don't regard ventilation as a glamorous feature. However, it is one of the most important—not only for preserving the good looks of your new room but for your safety and health. When installing a range hood, keep in mind that manufacturers recommend a maximum distance of 21 to 30 inches between the cooktop and the bottom of the hood in order to get the best ventilation. The hood should also be slightly longer and wider than the cooking surface.

An alternative to a system that uses a hood is down-draft ventilation, which is often installed in conjunction with an island cooktop or grill. The vent is in the countertop and the fan is below it. Down-draft venting works by forcing the air above the burners through a filter, then moving it out of the house via ductwork that runs to the outdoors. This method is not as effective as a hooded system, but it is more effective than a ductless fan.

Both hooded and nonhooded systems require a powerful fan. The more cooking you do, the more power you need—especially if you use high heat often (stir frying, for example). Check the air-movement rating of the fan for your unit (given in cubic feet per minute, or cfm). The National Kitchen and Bath Association (NKBA) recommends a minimum of 150 cfm per linear foot of cooking area (normally 3 to 4 feet) for cooktops or ranges installed against a wall and 180 cfm per linear foot for cooktops or grills installed in an island. Commercial-style equipment requires a fan with a rating about three times higher (1,200- to 1,800-cfm) because the heat it generates is higher. Long runs of ductwork necessitate a fan with greater power. In general, keep ductwork as short as possible. Calculating specific needs can be complicated, so consult your contractor.

smart tip

HOODLESS

Hoodless downdraft ventilation can be used with island cooktops if a hooded system is not possible. Downdraft ventilation forces the air above the burners through a filter, then out of the house via ductwork that is located below the floor in a crawlspace or basement. It's not as effective as a hooded system but an improvement over a ductless fan, which cannot do a proper job of removing nasty odors and expelling smoke and grease.

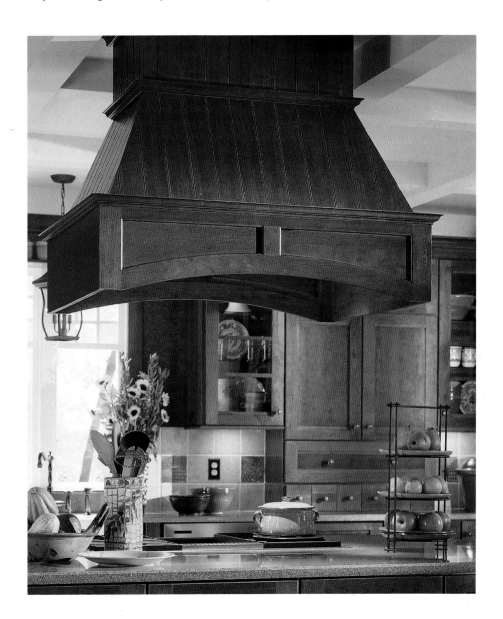

LEFT
This contemporary kitchen features built-in stainless-steel appliances and a smooth ceramic-glass cooktop. The homeowners chose a hood for over the cooktop that is as sleek in appearance as the rest of the appliances.

ABOVE
A custom-finished hood over a gas cooktop located in an island counter is enclosed in wood paneling that has been stained to match the kitchen's cabinets.

design workbook
A RANGE OF HOOD DESIGNS

plainly stated

Unadorned but handsome in brushed stainless steel, this ducted range hood fits in perfectly with the simple yet elegant design of the room and coordinates with the large professional range that has been installed within the large island. The metal also blends well with the cool blue hue on the walls and the white cabinetry's satin-finished chrome hardware.

a cooking "hearth"

A custom-finished hood completes a recessed cooking hearth in an Old World-inspired kitchen, top left. Special molding, stained to match the room's cabinets, adds a rich detail.

a unique look

Bead board and an embossed fish motif add a one-of-a-kind look to the housing for this venting system, left.

refrigerators and freezers

A refrigerator/freezer has a life expectancy of about 15 years, so if yours is approaching that mark or if it is more than 10 years old, you'd be wise to replace it. Today's more-efficient models can save up to 50 percent more energy than ones made in the early 1980s. And not only will a new refrigerator save energy, it will also provide better storage with flexible interior space that can be reconfigured and tailored to your needs. Shelves move up and down easily and extra-deep door bins can even accommodate a gallon container.

Typical full-size refrigerators range from 8 to 30 cubic feet. What size is right for you? It depends on how many people live in your house. Conventional wisdom recommends allocating 12 cubic feet for two people in a household and another 2 cubic feet for each additional person. Increase the total by another 2 cubic feet if you entertain often. That's the formula, but not all lifestyles fit neatly into it. If you eat out more than once or twice a week or shop daily for food, you don't need that much storage. If you have teenage children, shop in bulk, buy large containers of soda, juice, and milk, and frequently require space for large party platters, you'll need a refrigerator that is roomy enough to accommodate these considerations.

Your analysis should come down to common sense. If your family regularly eats fresh fruits and vegetables, a roomy crisper should be on your list of must-haves. If they eat cold meats and cheese, you'll want a separate drawer for those items. Do you precook meals for the week or buy frozen foods? If so, shop for a model with a generous freezer compartment. If you have extra-large freezing needs, consider buying an additional stand-alone freezer. As you make your selection, keep in mind that the fuller a refrigerator or freezer, the less it costs to run. So don't waste energy dollars with one that is too large for either your household or the amount of food you keep on hand. Keep any refrigerator at least two-thirds full for maximum efficiency.

Refrigerator sizes vary by more than capacity. Traditionally, units have protruded beyond the full depth of a base cabinet. As kitchen design has become sleeker, manufacturers have responded with 24-inch-deep models that fit snugly into a corresponding-size opening in a run of cabinetry for a built-in appearance. (Refrigerators can be finished with trim kits or custom panels to match your cabinets.) But as refrigerators have become shallower, they have also become wider to make up for lost storage capacity. Width varies greatly, so check the appliance's spec sheet when you're allocating space on the layout. Most conventional

OPPOSITE

You can have your cabinetmaker create custom panels for your refrigerator. This side-by-side model blends unobtrusively into the kitchen because it has been finished in this way.

ABOVE

Large models, like these separate freezer and refrigerator units, are built-in so that they do not extend into the room or beyond the front of the cabinetry. Built-in models are slightly less deep than freestanding ones.

refrigerators come in one of three styles: with a freezer on top, with a freezer on the bottom, or with the refrigerator and freezer side by side. There are also a number of optional features offered with today's refrigerators, including water-purifying systems with through-the-door water and ice, slide-out shelves, zoned temperature control, automatic ice makers, wine racks, front venting, see-through bins and adjustable drawers, wine caddies, door alarms, automatic defrosting, and on-the-door shelves and separate meat, cheese, and butter keepers.

■ **Top-Mounted Freezer.** The freezer compartment is on the top and is completely separate from the refrigerator. This is the most energy-efficient style because cold air from the freezer migrates down into the refrigerator and helps cool that section. These may be available with an optional through-the-door ice and water dispenser.

■ **Bottom-Mounted Freezer.** A bottom-freezer configuration (photo at right) locates a separate freezer compartment below the refrigerator. Its style does not allow for a through-the-door ice and water dispenser, but refrigerated foods are at a more comfortable height: you don't have to bend to get to the fruit bin or to the bottom door shelves.

Deciding between a top- or bottom-mounted refrigerator depends on which section—freezer or refrigerator—you want to be more accessible.

■ **Side-by-Side Refrigerator/Freezer.** This style offers the greatest access to both compartments and requires the least door-swing clearance in front. However, unless you're installing a 48-inch-wide model, typically narrow shelves may not handle bulky items like a turkey or a frozen pizza. This style is usually available with an optional through-the-door ice and water dispenser and a drop-down shelf that allows you access to items stored inside on the door. Both features save energy because they cut down on opening the door.

■ **Modular Refrigerators.** Under-counter refrigerators may solve some design difficulties and provide storage for specialized needs, such as chilling soft beverages or wine at an island or peninsula that serves as a bar or buffet. The concept of modular refrigeration and freezer drawers is quickly gaining popularity, making a logical argument for point-of-use storage and refrigeration in larger kitchens with multiple work triangles. Imagine keeping the vegetables in a refrigerated compartment right under the counter where you rinse and chop them. These modular units fit neatly under standard counters and come with drawer dividers and their own temperature-control devices, which let you make adjustments for vegetables, milk, and meat. If you are thinking about installing modular refrigeration, consult your contractor

and the manufacturers' spec sheets for information on plumbing and electrical requirements.

Commercial Refrigerators

You may like the way some commercial units look, with glass doors or an all stainless-steel appearance, but they really make no sense for residential use. If your family is like most, it spills and splashes its share of juices, sauces, and other liquids inside the refrigerator. Can you live with that mess showing through a glass door? Do you have the time to keep after it? On the other might be another option for anyone who can't sacrifice cabinet space but has the floor space to store one. Can you spare a drawer? Then go for a drawer-size unit; put one in the pantry or near the bar.

Waste-Disposal Units

Disposal units shred organic wastes and send them down the drain. Some communities require waste-disposal units; others ban them. Check with your local building department before deciding whether to install one.

A continuous-feed disposal unit allows you to feed waste into the mechanism as it operates. A batch-feed unit grinds up to 1½ to 2 quarts at a time. Continuous-feed models are controlled by a wall switch, batch-feed models by a built-in switch activated by replacing the drain lid. Batch-feed models are safer to use but more expensive. Local codes may dictate which type you can buy. Although waste-disposal units make a lot of noise, newer models operate more quietly. The life expectancy is about 10 years.

Trash Compactors

If you live in a community that charges by the bag for removing garbage, you'll appreciate the savings a trash compactor may offer.

Inside the appliance, a screw-driven ram compresses inorganic debris—cans or bottles, for example—to about 25 percent of their original volume. Compactors come in slide-out or drop-front models that range in size from 12 to 18 inches wide. Some models stand alone, but a well-planned kitchen can incorporate a compactor that is built-in and finished to match the cabinetry. Compactors don't use much electricity, but most require

OPPOSITE LEFT
Like other kitchen appliances, dishwashers can be installed to fit flush with the cabinets and covered with custom panels or left alone like this unit with a stainless-steel door.

OPPOSITE RIGHT
Similar to modular refrigeration, dishwasher drawers take up less space in the kitchen. They cost considerably more than a full-size dishwasher but can fit into a room's decor beautifully. This pair has been trimmed in plastic laminate.

ABOVE
In addition to the dishwasher drawers that are to the left of the sink, a trash compactor features a specially made bead-board front panel. The overall finished look of the sink area, including these appliances, appears unfitted and furniture-like.

smart tip TWO DISHWASHERS

Sometimes two is better than one. If you have the need (yours is a large household, you do a lot of cooking and baking, or you entertain often), two dishwashers make sense. That way, when one is full, you won't have to pile the sink with dirty dishes, pots, and pans. If you don't have space for a second full-size model, consider a dishwasher drawer.

special heavy-duty bags. Extras you may want to consider include a fan, deodorizer, safety lock, and quiet motor. You can expect a trash compactor to last about 10 years.

Hot-Water Dispensers

These handy devices heat ⅓ or ¼ gallon of water at a time and hold it at a bubbling 190 degrees Fahrenheit—an ideal temperature for making tea, coffee, or soup. (See Chapter Four, "The Best Materials," beginning on page 72.) While the main components fit under the sink, the dispenser tap may attach to the hole in the sink deck originally intended for the sprayer or through a hole in the countertop, with water lines running through any cabinet wall. The device's heating element requires access to an electrical line under the counter.

Coffee Stations

Coffee drinking seems to never have been more popular than it is today. No wonder some people are choosing to incorporate a built-in coffee machine into their new kitchen. Several manufacturers offer these appliances, which require plumbing.

smart steps
shopping tips

■ ## Step 1 TRY IT OUT
Ask for an in-store demonstration. You want the appliance to perform with space-age precision, but you shouldn't have to be an aeronautical engineer to use it. Also, check knobs and key pads. They should be within convenient reaching distance (on the front or side of the appliance) and easy to read, and they should accommodate any finger size—from a teenager's to an adult man's.

■ ## Step 2 LOOK FOR EASY CARE
You want to enjoy the new kitchen, but you won't if it's drudgery to keep it sparkling. Inquire about the finish and care—inside and out—of every appliance you purchase. For example, a stainless-steel finish on the exterior of an appliance tends to show fingerprints and smudges, but inside a refrigerator or dishwasher it's the most practical finish to keep clean. All it needs is an occasional sponging with water and a nonabrasive cleanser. And if you hate scrubbing an oven, it may be worth the extra amount (about $100) for one with a self-cleaning feature.

■ ## Step 3 MAKE SURE IT'S EFFICIENT
Manufacturers are required by law to label every appliance with certain energy-related information. That information must include a description of the appliance, the model number, projected energy costs to run the appliance, a range of energy costs for similar models, and a table to estimate energy costs for running the appliance based on local utility rates.

■ ## Step 4 MAKE SURE IT WILL FIT
Don't find out after the appliance has been delivered that it's too wide for its allocated location. Always check the measurements on your plan against the manufacturer's specifications and the actual in-store model, if possible. Another measurement to check is the depth of an appliance, especially if you want the look of something that is built-in. Some "cabinet-depth" refrigerators now come 24 inches deep, for example.

Step 5 THINK AHEAD

Will the refrigerator you purchase now serve you adequately for the next dozen years? Do you intend to be cooking more or less? If you anticipate that your household will increase or decrease in size within the next few years, you may want to reevaluate the size of any new appliance models you plan to purchase and upgrade or downgrade accordingly.

Step 6 CONFIRM DELIVERY DATES

It takes a lot of patience to live through a remodeling project. You'll most likely have to do without a kitchen for what will seem like an eternity during the remodeling itself. Knowing this, the last thing you want to face is a job that's complete except for an undelivered appliance. Extended delivery times often apply to European appliances, but even if everything you order is American-made, be sure to coordinate the completion of various stages of the work with the arrival of new equipment. You should go over this with your general contractor.

OPPOSITE BOTTOM
A hot-water-on-demand tap, which is situated to the left of this faucet, dispenses hot—but not boiling—water instantly.

ABOVE
If you decide to have special appliance panels created by your cabinet maker, factor that cost into your budget. If your cabinets are not custom made, it may be difficult to create an exact match.

LEFT
Fool the eye with refrigerator drawers finished to coordinate with the cabinets.

7

lighting the kitchen

WINDOWS   LIGHTING BASICS   DESIGN WORKBOOK   LIGHTBULBS
WHAT TO USE WHERE   SELECTING FIXTURES

Light. You know your kitchen needs it, but do you know how to get the type and the proper amount? Old blue fluorescents are a thing of the past. And thank goodness. Do you remember when modern kitchen lighting consisted of one fluorescent fixture in the middle of the ceiling? It made a strange humming sound and spilled an eerie bluish color around the room. Over the past few decades, technology has become more sophisticated, as has society's appreciation of the role of good lighting in design. There is probably no other room in the house that serves as many different needs as today's kitchen, and therefore it needs proper lighting to make it more welcoming and efficient. This chapter explores the various types of lighting, beginning with natural light, and how to use each effectively.

Plan your kitchen to include natural light spilling in through windows or skylights, as well as artificial light supplied by fixtures.

No real estate agent has ever heard a homeowner complain about too much natural light. Sunlight is so cheerful, it makes people feel good. When it streams into a room, it makes everything look better, too. With today's window technology, you can bring as much sunlight into your home as you like, and at the same time depend upon enhanced glazing options and low-E glass to solve the problem of energy-inefficient windows.

On the style side, windows previously associated with custom designs, such as the "architectural" styles popular today, are now available in standard sizes. Replacing an uninspired window with a graceful arch-top design is relatively easy and affordable. In fact, it's not difficult to change the entire architectural look of your kitchen by replacing the windows. Want to transform a 50-year-old space into a stylish contemporary setting? Use sleek casement-style units. Looking for a way to add vintage character? Install double-hung windows with snap-in muntins that imitate true divided-light windows. For drama, group individual casement or awning windows in an interesting formation along one wall. Where there is no place for a window, install an operable skylight, or roof window.

In a country kitchen, a garden window makes a display for plants and a spot to grow herbs year-round. There are also "art" styles, such as stained- and leaded-glass units, that enhance decorative styles, such as Arts and Crafts or French Country.

When considering a replacement window for the kitchen, it's important to keep in mind the architectural style both of the exterior of the house and of the other windows. If you choose a look that's different, select one that's compatible. Windows are placed on the exterior of a house in a pattern. If you change either the window style or pattern of placement in a room, you may inadvertently create an eyesore on the outside.

As you consider window placement in the kitchen, also take a look at the view you will have. Will it create a pleasant focal point or will you face the neighbor's shed? Also consider the direction the window faces in terms of the sun throughout the day. While a southern exposure offers the most sunlight, your kitchen may get hot—especially during summer—unless the window is covered. A northern exposure is cool and casts the quality of light that's desirable in an artist's studio but not in a breakfast nook. For early morning sunshine, an eastern exposure is best. Windows that face west receive lots of light in the late afternoon, which may need light or heat control.

window styles

Fixed

Snap-In Muntins

Casement

Awning

Double Hung

OPPOSITE
Study the available options, and choose windows that will not only bring in light and air but add architectural interest. These tall casements, topped by square units, frame an attractive view, too.

lighting basics

A rtificial lighting is the easiest way to set or change the atmosphere of an entire room. With one switch, your kitchen can go from a bright, efficient hub of activity to a softly lit setting for a quiet meal. Plus, the right light can make meal preparation and cleanup safer and more efficient. Just think how much time you might save if you could open a cabinet and spot whatever you need right away, or how quickly you could chop an onion in a bright, clear, shadowless space. In addition, performing tasks that sometimes feel like drudgery seems easier in the right light because your eyes are less susceptible to strain. The key to devising a versatile plan that can change with each activity, as well as with the time of day, begins with knowing about the different types of artificial light.

Ambient Light

Ambient, or general, light is illumination that fills an entire room. The source is sometimes an overhead fixture or group of fixtures, but the light itself does not appear to come from any specific direction. The most obvious example is fluorescent strips; the covering over the strips hides the source and diffuses the light.

A wall sconce is another example of ambient light. The fixture washes light up or down the wall for an overall glow. The wall reflects the light and diminishes the look of a single source. You can tell the light is coming from the sconce, but the overall glow is diffused.

The key to good ambient lighting is making it inconspicuous. It is merely the backdrop for the rest of the room, not the main feature. It always provides light but should never become obvious. Ambient lighting used during the day should blend with the natural light that enters a room. During the evening, you should be able to diminish or soften the light level so it doesn't contrast jarringly against the blackness outside.

RIGHT
While there are no visible decorative fixtures in this kitchen, there is still plenty of artificial light brightening work areas and the collection of pottery jugs is attractively showcased.

Task Light

Task light is purely functional. It should always be included as part of the lighting plan for any room, illuminating specific areas for specific jobs, such as reading a recipe or rolling out dough in a baking center. It's also essential for safety in a kitchen, especially when working around a hot stove or oven or using sharp instruments. The key to good task lighting is installing it directly over or slightly to the side of each work surface. Small lights mounted to the underside of a cabinet are an excellent example of well-thought placement. If you placed the light sources directly overhead, your body would create shadows as you bend over the work surface.

Task lighting is intended for more than just the countertop. Include it in every area of the room where you work—at the cook-top, over the sink, at the desk, above the laundry and ironing center, even above the snack bar and table. Install a separate switch for task lights; don't include them on the switch that controls the general lighting for the room. With task lighting, the ideal is to be able to turn it on and off easily whenever you need it.

Accent Light

Often the most overlooked element in any room but always the most dramatic, accent light draws attention to a particular element, such as an interesting architectural feature or decorative object. The key here is choosing what to highlight. Don't light every object at once or they'll compete with each other. Look at the best features of your kitchen—whether built-in or decorative—and decide what underpins the overall look you want to achieve. Use accent light to add personality to the room. Light a

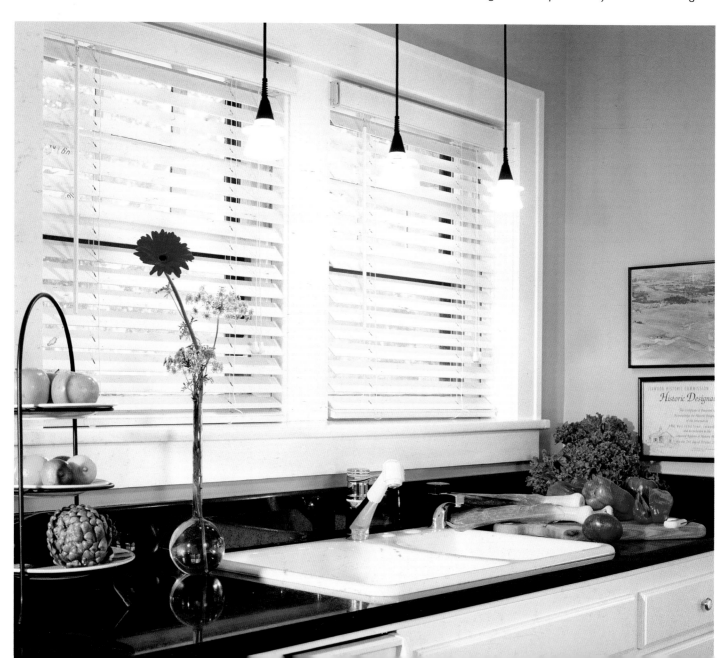

cooking alcove or focus attention on a handsome custom range hood. Install recessed light fixtures within a ceiling cove. Show off pretty stemware inside a glass-door cabinet by mounting small lights inside the cabinet box. Highlight a pottery or basket collection on top of cabinets with small lamps that can be masked behind crown molding. Spotlight wall art.

Accent light is purely optional, but without it there is no focus, no character to the space. With it, however, a room becomes an exciting, theatrical, and rich environment.

Decorative Light

While accent light draws attention to another object or surface, decorative light draws attention to itself. It can be kinetic, in the form of candles or the glow from inside a fireplace, or static, such as a fixed wall candelabra. It doesn't highlight specific areas the way accent light does, and it doesn't provide a great deal of illumination as does ambient light, but decorative light is the device most designers love to use. Its sole purpose is to grab attention: lighting for the sake of lighting. Because it commands notice, however, it can be used indirectly to distract from something else. In this sense, it can be functional, as well. You can use decorative lighting in the kitchen to draw the eye upward toward a cathedral ceiling or to distract attention from the mess at the food preparation area. For example, candlelight on the table at dinnertime will keep everyone from noticing the pots and pans piled in the sink. By capturing your eye, decorative lighting forces your focus away from everything else.

Some sources of decorative light include candles, chandeliers, neon sculptures or signs, a strip of miniature lights—any type of light that is deliberate and contrived. Include this form of lighting to strike a balance among all lighting in the room, including natural light from the sun and moon.

OPPOSITE
There are many ways to provide essential task lighting. Here, attractive decorative fixtures illuminate the sink and surrounding countertops, which is the most used work center in any kitchen.

ABOVE
Provide sufficient task lighting with lamps built right into the range hood and a series of undercabinet fixtures to brighten the adjoining work surfaces.

design workbook
LIGHTING FOR THE SERIOUS COOK

multiply the effect

Serious cooks demand superior lighting, especially in all task areas. Here, the pale color of the upper cabinets, the countertop, and the stainless-steel surfaces reflect light, which helps to brighten the space.

add safety and drama

Recessed fixtures installed above the range provide enough ambient light for moving about the space. Lighting installed behind opaque doors turns a necessity into a dramatic element and illuminates the unit's interior. (See also top left.)

bring a dash of color

Manufacturers offer a wide array of colorful, decorative pendants, left. These work equally well as task, accent, or ambient light. But hang them high enough so that they do not encroach on work areas below.

lightbulbs

ifferent types of bulbs, or "lamps" as lighting professionals call them, can affect the way your kitchen looks, feels, and functions. Does this mean you can change a few lightbulbs and forget about your remodeling project? Not likely. But you can make dramatic changes in your kitchen by switching from one type of bulb to another.

Understanding the differences in lamps will help you select the right light source for every area of your kitchen. Light is like paint: you can get different effects depending on the combinations of bulbs and fixtures you use. And color is nothing but a reflection of different wavelengths of light energy. When selecting lamps for your kitchen, always consider the relationship between color and light and what it is you want to illuminate, whether it is an object, a surface, or an area.

Standard Measurements for Color

Scales used in universal lighting assess the color temperature that a lamp gives off and how light from the lamp affects the objects it lights. The term *color temperature* describes the appearance of light in terms of the warmth or coolness of its color. Fluorescent lamps, which do not emit a continuous spectrum of light, are assigned a *correlated color temperature* (CCT) value. Lamps, which range from red to orange to yellow to blue to blue-white, are designated in color according to the Kelvin (K) temperature scale. This will help you select lamps that are closely matched. You will also be able to vary coolness or warmth. Generally, light sources that are rated below 3,000K are considered warm, while those above 4,100K are perceived as cool. The recommended range for light sources should fall between 3,000 and 3,500K.

Color rendition describes how a light source affects the perception of the color of an object it illuminates. The Color Rendition Index (CRI) is a way of measuring a specific lamp's ability to render true color (the color of an object in sunlight). The color-rendering capabilities of lamps are rated from 1 to 100, with true color at 100.

Types of Bulbs

Most homes include a combination of warm and cool tones, so selecting bulbs that provide balanced lighting close to what appears normal to the eye is usually the most attractive choice. Experiment with balancing various combinations of bulbs to create the desired effect. To help you achieve the balance you want, here is a brief description of the different types of bulbs.

■ **Incandescent.** Like sunlight, incandescent bulbs emit continuous-spectrum light, or light that contains every color. Illumination from these bulbs, in fact, is even warmer than sunlight, making its effect very appealing. It makes skin tones look good and enhances the feeling of well-being. Also, the bulbs come in a variety of shapes, sizes, and applications. One type even features a waterproof lens cover that makes it suitable for use near a sink or above the cooktop where steam can gather. Incandescent bulbs may be clear, diffuse, tinted, or colored, and they may have a reflective coating inside. The drawback is that incandescents use a lot of electricity and produce a lot of heat. That means they'll cost a lot more energy dollars to run.

■ **Fluorescent.** These energy-efficient bulbs cast a diffuse, shadowless light that makes them great for general illumination. They are economical, but the old standard fluorescents produce an unflattering light, making everything and everyone appear bluish and bland. Newer fluorescent bulbs, called triphosphor fluorescent lamps, are warmer and render color that more closely resembles sunlight. Fluorescents are available both in the familiar tube versions and in newer, compact styles. Mixing these bulbs with incandescent lamps, plus adding as much natural light to the kitchen plan as possible, can make fluorescents more appealing. Be aware, though, that in some parts of the country local codes require installing fluorescent lights—no other types—to conform to energy conservation mandates.

■ **Halogen.** This is actually a type of incandescent lamp that produces a brighter, whiter light at a lower wattage, with greater energy efficiency. The disadvantages are a higher price tag and higher heat output that requires special shielding. However, although halogens cost more up front, they last longer than conventional incandescents. A subcategory of halogen is the low-voltage version. It produces a 50-percent brighter light than standard halogen and is even more energy efficient. Compact in size, low-

voltage halogens are typically used for creative accent lighting.

■ **Fiber Optics.** One of countless innovations gradually finding its way into the home, a fiber-optic system consists of one extremely bright lamp to transport light to one or more destinations through fiber-optic conduits. Used to accent spaces, fiber-optic lighting has the advantage of not generating excessive heat. This makes it ideal as an alternative to decorative neon lights, which get very hot and consume a great deal of energy.

BELOW
Fixtures that use incandescent bulbs, or "lamps," as they are known in the trade, provide the perfect light for dining.

what to use where

When a room isn't bright enough, most people just exchange low-watt bulbs for high-watt versions. Wattage, however, is simply a measurement of how much electricity a lamp consumes. The light output of a bulb is actually measured in lumens. If the bulbs you have been using aren't providing enough general light, substitute them with ones that have more lumens. The next time you shop for bulbs, read the packaging, which indicates the lumens per watt (lpw) produced by a bulb. The more lumens per watt, the more efficient the lamp. When looking for intensity produced by a lamp, refer to its candlepower (Cp). The more candela (units), the brighter the source.

But when planning a suitable light design, you must take other factors into consideration, too. Before you do anything about buying lamps and fixtures, assess how you will use the kitchen in addition to the basic functions of cooking, eating, and cleaning up. Think about how you want it to feel—perhaps cool and efficient while you work but cozy while you dine.

Assess the reflectance levels in the room—the amount of light reflected from a colored surface, such as a tiled countertop or painted wall. Light colors and shiny surfaces are reflective, dark colors and matte surfaces are absorbent. For example, white reflects 80 percent of the light in a room, while black reflects only 4 percent. When selecting materials and colors, therefore, remember that a kitchen with light walls and cabinets and high-gloss countertops and flooring requires less light than one with dark or matte-finished surfaces and wood cabinetry.

Next in your evaluation, consider the size of the room. How high are the ceilings? Tall ceilings require brighter lights to dispel shadows. But you'll have to tone down the brightness in a room with low ceilings because light bounces off low ceilings and walls. The number of windows in the room will also affect your kitchen's lighting needs. Do the windows face the sunny south, or is the kitchen exposure directed toward the north or somewhere in between?

Designers typically determine lighting needs by using suggested foot-candle (Fc) levels for different activities and areas. Foot-candles, which refer to the amount of light that falls on a surface, are used primarily for directional lamps. To determine the foot-candle power you will need to adequately light an area, divide the candlepower (Cp) of the bulb you intend to use by the distance (D) from the fixture to the surface squared ($Fc = Cp \div D^2$).

There are no perfect stock formulas. But by looking at how each of these factors affects the others, you can make educated choices when developing your lighting plan. Keeping in mind the science and technology involved in lighting will help you determine your lighting requirements for the new kitchen. Ideally, you will want to incorporate a variety of the available options for various activities in order to create the desired ambiance and decorative effects. Use the following steps to get started.

OPPOSITE
A well-lit interior allows the china and glassware stored in this display cabinet to be seen at its sparkling best.

RIGHT
Here, pendant fixtures provide a warm glow in the bar area of a kitchen designed for entertaining.

smart steps
devise a plan

■ Step 1 EXAMINE YOUR ACTIVITIES

Make a list of everything that occurs in your kitchen on a daily basis. Besides typical kitchen duties, such as cooking meals and cleaning up, include your hobby or craft pursuits and anything else you do—or would like to do—in the kitchen, such as clipping coupons, reading the paper, or sewing. Be sure to consult other family members. Undoubtedly, there will be lots of things on your list, which only makes the lighting choices more critical. If your list gets too long, group similar tasks.

■ Step 2 SKETCH AN INFORMAL PLAN

Refer to your base map or start with a new drawing. (Working on a piece of tissue paper that has been taped over your base map will do fine, too.) If your remodeling project encompasses adjoining rooms or is part of an open plan, add those areas to your sketch and design one cohesive lighting plan that flows from one space to the next. Circle all activity centers on your map: cooking and cleanup zones; baking center; garden and crafts areas; and so on.

Every task and function you do will require a different light level. For example, you'll need bright, clear light near the chopping block but something less intense at the snack bar. And don't forget to include different types of light as well as the ability to adjust the intensity of the level of light in your design.

You will mark each circle with a G for general or ambient light, T for task light, A for accent light, and D for decorative light. In some places, you may want to indicate more than one. For example, if you plan on using your kitchen table for small intimate dinners and paying the bills, you might indicate A, G, and T. Identify your general lighting needs first, and then add your task lighting. Mark the spots for accent and decorative lighting on your plan last.

Even though some forms of decorative light don't require installation (candles, for example), indicate them on your plan because they will interact at times with other types of light in your kitchen.

While energy-efficient fluorescent lighting is mandated by code in some regions for kitchen remodelings, it is an excellent choice for general lighting because these lamps often remain on for hours at a time. To select fluorescent bulbs most flattering to foods, look for those with warmer tones, represented by 3,000K to 3,500K on the light index.

Now you're ready to place your general lighting. The rule for spacing general light is to create a consistent spread of light. If your light breaks into noticeable patterns, the sources are placed too far apart. Depending

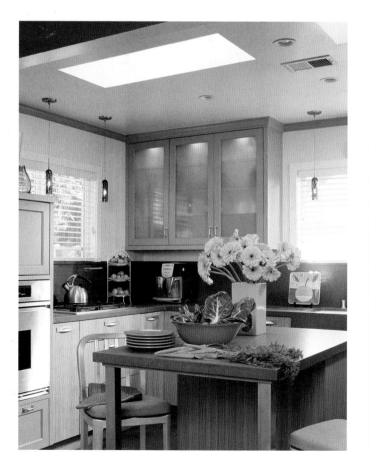

LEFT
Don't overlook sources for bringing in natural daylight. If there is no space for a new window, consider a skylight to brighten your space—particularly important if you use the kitchen during daylight hours.

OPPOSITE
Be sure your lighting plan includes sufficient fixtures. The aim is to provide a consistent spread of light without any overly bright or dark areas anywhere in the room.

on your arrangement of cabinets, general lights may be most effective if installed near work areas rather than in the center of the ceiling. Two 48-inch fluorescent tubes in one fixture are sufficient for kitchens that measure up to 120 square feet. For larger kitchens, use fixtures that accommodate four 48-inch tubes.

Recessed incandescent fixtures also provide general illumination and can be dimmed; recessed down-light fluorescent fixtures placed 6 to 8 feet apart provide the best light spread. Recessed incandescent fixtures spaced the same way also provide good general illumination for the kitchen.

In large kitchens, you might try perimeter lighting. Plan for two-tube recessed or surface-mounted fluorescent fixtures in the ceiling, over the front edge of the counter to form a square, L-, or U-shaped pattern to conform to your cabinet layout and provide general illumination. An alternative is to install recessed floodlights or fluorescent tubes in the soffit area (if there is one) above the cabinets.

Next, indicate task lighting on your plan. Your new kitchen may include special areas not related to food preparation and cleanup, but here are the typical places in every kitchen that will need illumination.

■ **Sinks.** An individual recessed down light or fixture that can be outfitted with an energy-efficient compact fluorescent lamp provides adequate task lighting when installed in the ceiling or soffit over the sink. Two incandescent down lights placed 18 inches apart on a 2-foot track or recessed and centered over the sink are also effective. Another solution is to use a thin-line fluorescent tube, which can be unobtrusively mounted behind an 8-inch face board.

■ **Ranges.** Most range hoods are equipped with fixtures that accommodate a 40- or 60-watt incandescent bulb or its equivalent, which is required for efficiency. For economy in general task lighting, substitute compact or linear fluorescent fixtures for incandescents where possible. Position any task light toward the front of the range to prevent glare, following directions given for lighting the sink area.

■ **Countertops.** Under-cabinet lighting is ideal for countertops. Mount fixtures as close to the front of the cabi-

net as possible to prevent reflected glare. Choose from slim energy-efficient fluorescents, miniature track lights, or low-voltage linear systems, all of which are suitable. Use an opaque fixture or shield on the cabinet bottom to minimize glare. If you use fluorescent tubes, install them to cover at least two-thirds of the length of the counter.

■ **Peninsulas and counters without upper cabinets.** In a small kitchen, the general lighting fixture over the counter will have to double as a task light. If you have the space, recess or surface-mount fixtures 20 inches apart, centered over the counter. For this area, use 75-watt reflector floodlights or equivalent compact fluorescent lamps or miniature low-voltage pendants.

■ **Islands or booths.** One or more decorative pendants are suitable for use. Installed with dimmers, these lights provide atmosphere perfect for dining. Figure on a total of about 120 watts incandescent or 32 to 40 watts fluorescent to light a booth. Miniature, low-voltage pendants equipped with tiny halogen bulbs add a contemporary look.

■ Lighting over the table. In a kitchen with a conventional 8-foot-high ceiling, install a fixture so that its bottom is 27 to 36 inches above the table. Raise it 3 inches for every additional foot of ceiling height. With a chandelier, consider the height of the backs of the dining chairs when deciding how high to place it. Place the fixture higher for tall ladderback chairs; install it lower for short captain's chairs. Chandeliers or pendants with down lights bring out the sparkle in tableware, especially crystal. Bulbs totaling 200 to 300 watts are sufficient to light most tables, but a minimum of 150 watts is needed. For up lighting, experiment with decorative bulbs; clear or frosted bulbs are handsome with materials such as wood or wrought iron, while incandescent or amber bulbs in traditional fixtures give the impression of candlelight.

With a pendant fixture, there should be an open top to provide upward light. Underneath, a diffusing bowl, disk, or semi-opaque bulb will help eliminate any glare. Make sure the bulb does not extend below the edge of the shade.

If your kitchen table has a glass top, your fixture's reflection may produce unpleasant glare. Augment or replace chandelier lighting with track or recessed fixtures. Use a ring of four down lights around the table's edge or on each side of the centered chandelier over a long table. Smaller recessed housings are effective, and low-voltage recessed lighting can create an appealing ambiance especially when used with a dimmer, which will let you control brightness.

Step 3 CHECK YOUR LOCAL CODE

Every municipality has strict regulations regarding the type of fixtures you can use and the placement of light and electricity around water. If you want to pass inspection, be sure you don't violate codes by specifying a lamp that isn't allowed in your area or by installing a fixture too close to an area that's exposed to water.

Step 4 VISIT LIGHTING SHOWROOMS

The best way to learn about your options is to visit lighting showrooms. You can often take advantage of free in-store consultations. If your plan is complicated or if you have questions that require at-home consultation, you may be pleasantly surprised at the modest fee charged by a lighting specialist.

OPPOSITE
Provide at least 150 watts of light to illuminate an eating area such as this. Bulbs that are too large and bright could create an unpleasant glare on reflective counter-top surfaces.

RIGHT
This drawing illustrates the proper placement of recessed fixtures for a glass table, located just off of the four table corners for a subtle effect.

selecting fixtures

There is practically an endless number of lighting-fixture styles designed to match any decor and catch everyone's imagination. The past few years have proved to be a lighting designer's dream, as fixtures have become more decorative and lighting schemes more varied and eclectic. From nostalgic reproductions to architecture-inspired designs and contemporary styles, fixtures suit any look, and take the form of wall sconces, chandeliers, pendants, recessed canister lights, track lights, ceiling fixtures, and novelty types—and they come in every finish imaginable.

OPPOSITE
Consider a chandelier to add sparkle and a warm glow to the eating area of a traditionally styled kitchen. This treatment requires another source, such as recessed high hats, to provide fill light for the space.

ABOVE
It's possible to find attractive pendant fixtures designed to suit every decorative style, from farmhouse to high-tech contemporary.

LEFT
Select distinctive fixtures that will not only add light but bring a pop of personality and some drama to your new kitchen. If the fixture is metal, try to match it with cabinet hardware.

The copious selection of finishes offers lots of excitement, too. Look for everything from enamels to brass, chrome, pewter, nickel, and copper, which can be brushed, matted, or antiqued. There are also vintage designs in wrought iron and verdigris. For added interest, select fixtures with a combination of finishes, such as verdigris with antique brass or copper paired with wrought iron. Whatever you choose, stick to a style that is compatible with other decorative elements in the room.

Anywhere family meals are eaten deserves good, convivial lighting. In addition, providing adequate task lighting, especially in the cooking area, where sharp knives, scalding and burning materials, and the subtleties of fine cooking coexist, only makes good sense. Accent lighting and decorative lighting can only add to your pleasure. The placement of fixtures may vary depending on the size of your kitchen. But above all, let your lighting needs dictate how many fixtures to buy and where to install them in your kitchen.

smart tip

GLARING ERRORS

Because kitchens contain so many surfaces that are highly reflective, such as polished stone, ceramic or glass tile, and stainless steel, you'll need to be careful not to create glare with the lighting you choose.

One area of concern is the undercabinet lighting designed to illuminate work areas on countertops. Make sure that anyone who is seated at a counter or table in line with the lighting is shielded from looking directly into the bulb. Choose models with opaque covers over the lamps. Or install a narrow molding on the bottom of the upper cabinets. Ask the electrician to provide switches so that the lighting in each area operates independently. And consider dimmers for maximum control.

OPPOSITE TOP
Because so many tasks, from food preparation to cleanup, take place at the sink, it's important to include some form of task lighting there.

ABOVE
Install a chandelier on a dimmer in the dining area to create a warm, convivial atmosphere at meal times.

LEFT
Glass globe fixtures provide a soft diffused light, that is emitted in all directions of the room.

RIGHT
Eliminate the possibility of glare by choosing a fixture with a glass insert that diffuses light.

8

focus on style

TRADITIONAL   CONTEMPORARY   COUNTRY COTTAGE   PROVENÇAL
SHAKER   ARTS AND CRAFTS   THE DECORATING PHASE

Most people spend a lot of time in the kitchen relaxing and socializing, perhaps even more than cooking and cleaning up. So take the time to decide how you want the room to look, what colors, fabrics, and textures you're drawn to, and the mood you'd like to create. If you're still weighing the warmth and casual feeling of country decor against the grace and formality of a traditional setting, examine some of the elements that make up different decorating styles. Look at art books, and pay close attention to furniture styles, which are influencing today's cabinet design. Think about favorite decorating themes from other rooms in the house that can be carried into the kitchen. In this chapter you'll get some style-specific ideas and learn how to create a decorating scheme for your kitchen that suits your taste and your lifestyle.

Plain white cabinets and stainless-steel appliances put a fresh face on country style. Blue backsplash tile adds subtle color.

gathering
ideas

When considering style, everyone needs inspiration. Forget the latest trends; rather, consider rooms you have admired and the features that attracted you. Was it a painted finish on the cabinetry? The color or pattern of the wallpaper or window treatment? A handsome wood floor? A pretty collection displayed in a hutch or on a wall? How did the room make you feel? Cheerful? Relaxed? Animated? Nostalgic? This is the kind of thinking that eventually results in a finished design you will never tire of and will continue to enjoy year after year.

In addition, look for clues in the rest your house. Study its architecture. Is it contemporary? Colonial? Victorian? An Arts and Crafts-style bungalow? Is there elaborate trimwork, or are the walls, doors, and windows streamlined and spare? Even if the architecture is nondescript, you can introduce a period flavor in the room with reproduction cabinets and fixtures, window treatments, wallpaper, and accessories. Is there a theme you have already established with furnishings and decoration? Do you like antiques or modern art? Are you a collector or someone who prefers pared-down space? You can build on these features and preferences or depart from them entirely. Just find one transitional element, such as the floor treatment or color scheme, to create a visual bridge so that the change from room to room isn't too abrupt. If your kitchen will open onto other areas, such as the family room, link the two spaces with related materials; for example, coordinate the fabric used for the family room's window treatment with the kitchen wallpaper.

Whatever you do, your approach to decorating the new kitchen should be deliberate. Let it evolve over time; don't rush your choices. Live with paint, tile, and wallpaper samples for a while. This chapter offers a brief description of popular decorating styles. Feel free to follow them or design a variation on one of these themes. The colors, patterns, and other materials offered are just suggestions. Refer to them as starting points, but let your own preferences be your guide in the end. If you're not sure about something, don't do it.

OPPOSITE
If you spend a lot of time in the kitchen, make sure it feels good; create an environment that pleases all of your senses. This pretty room would make anyone feel welcome.

ABOVE
Color is a major player in today's kitchen, whether it's used as an attention-grabbing detail or as a large bold statement. Teal blue is drop-dead gorgeous on these cabinets.

smart tip MIXING STYLES

An eclectic look is sophisticated but hard to pull off. Unless you are experienced in design and feel very confident about your choices, you may want to stick with one style. However, if you do want to try mixing them, keep in mind that some styles work well together while others do not. One look that never fails to appear dramatic is the pairing of traditional architecture with ultra-modern furnishings. Find common elements in different styles that will make them work together. Good examples of compatible looks include country and traditional or Shaker. In a contemporary setting, you can incorporate a few elements of one of these: Art Deco, Arts and Crafts, or Shaker style.

Traditional Style

Today's traditional style incorporates elements of English and American eighteenth- and early nineteenth-century design. Marked by symmetry and balance and enhanced by the look of fine-crafted details, it is dignified, rich, and formal.

Choose wood cabinetry finished with a cherry or mahogany stain or painted white, with details like fluted panels, bull's-eye corner blocks, and dentil and crown molding. For the door style, a raised cathedral panel (top slightly arched) is typical. An elegant marble countertop or a laminate faux version fit well here, as do hand-painted tiles. Polished brass hardware and fittings add an Old World touch.

Colors to consider include classic Wedgwood blue or deep jewel tones. Windows and French doors with true divided lights or double-hung units with pop-in muntins have great traditional-style appeal. Dress them with formal curtain panels or swags. Botanical-inspired patterns, formal stripes, and tapestry or crewelwork look-alikes can tie the room together.

Furnish this kitchen with an antique or reproduction hutch, where you can display formal china, and a table and chairs in traditional Windsor or Queen Anne style.

RIGHT
Furniture details and classical elements, such as crown moldings and fluted panels, underscore the formal look of this kitchen. The cabinets have been finished a warm antique white.

BELOW
Ornate brackets cared with the classic acanthus leaf motif almost appear to hold up the island's granite countertop. Actually, they are just decorative.

smart tip TRADITIONAL STYLE

You don't have to replace your kitchen cabinetry to get some of the fine furniture-quality details discussed above. Custom-made details will be expensive, but you can purchase prefabricated trims at local lumber mills and home centers. For example, crown molding, applied to the top of existing cabinetry and stained or painted to match the door style, may be all you need. Likewise, you can replace old hardware with reproduction polished-brass door and drawer knobs or pulls for a finishing touch.

design workbook
IN THE GOTHIC TRADITION

a style takes shape

Pointed arches on the cabinets and a rounded cathedral arch over the cooktop establish the Gothic style.

lighting with a theme

The chandelier, with electrified "candles" looks as if it could be from a medieval castle. (See also top left.)

creating a feeling

Stone tiles used for the recess behind the cook-top convey a sense of an ancient hearth and great hall.

following through

The faucets are simple in shape form and almost primitive in style. The matte bronze finish suggests age.

to the last detail

The small dia-mond-shape, carved out of the chair backs, is another true Gothic motif. (See also left.)

Contemporary Style

What's referred to as "contemporary" style evokes images of clean architectural lines; an absence of decoration and color; and materials such as stainless steel, chrome, glass, and stone. Indeed, its roots are at the turn of the last century, when architects and designers flatly rejected the exaggerated artificial embellishments of the Victorians by turning to natural products and pared-down forms. Various modern movements, evolving over the course of the industrialized twentieth century, gradually incorporated new man-made materials into their streamlined forms. Hence the high-tech look popularized in the 1970s and 1980s.

Today, contemporary style is taking a softer turn, even in the kitchen, a place where hard edges, cool reflective surfaces, and cutting-edge technology abound. Kitchen designers are taking another look at time-honored forms and giving them a new spin. It's not unusual to see updated versions of traditional fixtures and fittings or new uses for natural materials in a contemporary kitchen, especially as improved finishes make these products more durable and easier to maintain. And although black and white have been the classic mainstays in a contemporary room, the stark white palette of the last two decades has been replaced with earthy wood hues, bold color (especially on modern European-inspired designs), and warmer shades of white.

When selecting cabinets for your contemporary kitchen, pair a frameless door with a wood finish. Laminate cabinetry is still compatible with this style, but for an updated look, wood is it. Although a contemporary room is often monochromatic or neutral, don't be afraid to use color or to mix several materials or finishes, such as wood and metal. Combinations of wood and various metals—stainless steel, chrome, copper, brass, and pewter on surfaces like cabinet doors, countertops, and floors—make strong statements, as do stone and glass. Creative combinations like these keep the overall appearance of the room sleek but not sterile. For more visual interest, apply a glazed or textured finish to neutral-colored walls. And bring as much of the outdoors into this room as possible. Install casement-style windows, skylights, or roof windows to blend with contemporary architecture. Easy access to adjoining outdoor living spaces, such as decks or open-air kitchens, is highly desirable. For window treatments, Roman shades or vertical blinds offer a crisp, tailored look.

Stay with metals for lighting fixtures and hardware. Chrome, pewter, or nickel would work well. Keep your eye on function, not frills. The contemporary room revels in the pure architecture of the space.

Furnishings for a contemporary kitchen tend to have a sleek architectural look, too. In fact, much of what is considered classic contemporary furniture has been designed by well-known twentieth-century architects. Chair and table legs are typically straight, with no turnings or ornamentation. For a sophisticated look, mix complementary materials; for example, pair a glass table with upholstered chairs or a metal table with wood chairs. Display contemporary pottery on a shelf or inside a glass cabinet.

OPPOSITE
Geometric shapes always play a part in Modern design. Various neutral tones add relief to several banks of cabinetry in this open design.

ABOVE
Contemporary design has taken a warmer turn today. These cabinets feature a medium-tone wood that is complemented by the flooring and the tones in the granite counters.

smart tip CONTEMPORARY STYLE

Incorporate elements of Arts and Crafts, Art Deco, or other designs associated with the modern movements of the twentieth century; their clean, geometric lines are quite compatible with this environment. This eclectic approach can result in a sophisticated look. Shop for framed fine art prints, vintage-inspired wallpaper, reproduction hardware, faucets, or light fixtures to underscore your theme.

design workbook
CONTEMPORARY AND WARM

the versatile island

The center island doubles as a food preparation area and a place to enjoy a meal or keep the cook company.

cold storage

Freezer drawers, top left, are part of a custom-finished cooling and freezing system. (See also bottom left.)

straightforward look

Plain-panel wood doors and sleek chrome hardware, bottom far left, reinforce the kitchen's modern aesthetic.

unobtrusive cooking

On the other side of the island, there's a professional-style range and storage for pots, middle left.

customized cooling

Refrigeration is behind this door and the two drawers, bottom left, which were finished to match the cabinets.

Country Style

Whether you call it American, French, English, Italian, or Scandinavian, this style is always a favorite because of its basic, casual, relaxed feeling. In fact, every country has its own version. "Country" implies a deeper connection to the outdoors and the simple life than other styles and uses an abundance of natural elements. Start off with plain wood cabinetry stained a light maple, or add a distressed, crackled, or pickled finish. This is the perfect kitchen for mixing different finishes because unmatched pieces underpin the informal ambiance of a country room. Cabinet door styles are typically framed, sometimes with a raised panel. Beadboard cabinets are a typical American country choice. Or leave the doors off, allowing colorful dishes and canned and boxed goods to create a fun display. For the countertop, install butcher block or hand-painted or silk-screened tiles. Another option is a colorful or patterned countertop fabricated from inlaid solid-surfacing material. Also, consider concrete or stone. Once thought of as too modern for a country kitchen, these materials can blend in beautifully with an updated country sensibility. A working fireplace will add charm to your country kitchen, but a simple potted herb garden on the windowsill will, too.

Wood floors are a natural choice in this setting, whether they are real, engineered, or laminate. Terra-cotta tiles are also an attractive accent to a European-inspired country setting. Be sure to use throw rugs in front of the sink for added comfort.

For a custom touch, add a stenciled backsplash or wall border. Or try a faux finish like sponging, ragging, or combing. These techniques are fun and easy, and they add texture to your walls. For a Continental flavor, apply a glaze that imitates a rustic fresco finish. Use extra space to hang herbs for drying.

Install double-hung windows. (Standard casement windows look too contemporary in this setting.) Finish them with full trim, and dress them with simple cotton curtains.

ABOVE
A small antique table brings added charm to this updated country kitchen. When meals are not being served, it can be used as a worktable in lieu of a center island.

OPPOSITE
An oak floor and cabinets, open storage on cabinet shelves, and reproduction schoolhouse lamps suggest an old-fashioned country store.

smart tip COUNTRY STYLE

Keep it simple, and avoid cutesy clutter. A touch of whimsy is fine and always looks at home in a country kitchen, especially when it is handcrafted. One way to achieve a country look is with hardware. Pick up an accent color from the tile or wallpaper, and paint unfinished knobs and pulls, which are available at craft stores. Or mix and match standard metal or glass pieces with a few fun ones. Designs you might consider include fruit, vegetable, or animal motifs.

design workbook
COUNTRY BLUES

wide open spaces

This large layout leaves plenty of room for living. A painted country-blue floor adds adds the right homey touch.

playful pattern

Checkered tiles in blue and white, a country favorite, look cheerful on the backsplash. (See also top left.)

modern means

A professional-quality freezer-refrigerator and range serve the cook and this family-style kitchen well.

island work center

A butcher-block-topped island, bottom left, provides an additional work surface across from the sink.

tea for two or more

A vintage kitchen table and chairs is a great accent for the room and provides a place for small meals or casual dining.

The Cottage Look

This vintage look, inspired by quaint English-country style, is appealing in the kitchen because it's cozy, casual, and warm. Framed wood cabinets with an unfitted or unmatched appearance—especially in a mix of finishes, such as a honey maple paired with a color stain that looks aged or distressed—provide a good starting point for building on this theme. Muntin-glass doors and built-in open plate or pot racks and display shelves should be part of the cabinetry's design. Milk- or clear-glass knobs and pulls will dress the cabinets nicely, or use forged metal hardware for a rustic appearance.

Bead board on the walls always looks at home in this style kitchen, as does brick. Either material would make an attractive backsplash treatment. Paint or stain the bead board to complement the colors used in the room. An English import, the AGA cooker, is a great way to bring the old-time European look of a cast-iron stove into the room while providing all the modern-day conveniences. Install an exposed-apron (farmhouse-style) sink with a reproduction chrome and porcelain faucet set to add more charm. On the floor, use wide wood planks or stone with a colorful hand-painted floorcloth on top. Something with a pattern of big, chubby blooms would be attractive. Bring more color into the room with blue-green surfaces accented in varying shades of rose

and cream. Introduce vintage linens for added nostalgia.

A double-hung window lends a traditional note, but if you can make the style work with the exterior of your house, a Gothic-inspired architectural design would tie it all together. This style, with Medieval roots, was popular with the Victorians. Accent with lighting fixtures that resemble old-fashioned gas lamps or electrified candle sconces.

For furniture, include a good-size farmhouse table in your plan, as well as a Welsh dresser and plate rack for displaying a pretty collection of Majolica or similar earthenware.

LEFT
Just about anything goes in a cottage kitchen, which tends to have a playful look. Here, the owners installed refurbished vintage appliances and light fixtures and put their collections on display.

OPPOSITE
Sunflowers, a ceramic rooster, and mustard-color pottery are some of the accessories that can bring French country style to your kitchen.

Provençal Style

This French-country style evokes images of the Mediterranean and warm, sunny days. Its origins go back to the one- and two-room farmhouses of southern France built centuries ago, when the kitchen was a large communal room. To re-create its charming ambiance, whitewash walls or apply a subtle glaze finish in an earth tone, such as rose ocher or sienna. Install wood on the ceiling beams with an aged or distressed look.

Original Provençal kitchens had large limestone hearths and, of course, working fireplaces. Your modern-day version may or may not have a working fireplace, but you can introduce limestone by installing it on the floor. Otherwise, use rustic clay tiles, which also have a warm, earthy appeal. For the appearance of a hearth, design a cooking alcove to house the range or cooktop. Accent it with colorful tiles or brick. Create a focal point at the cooking area with a handsome copper range hood. Hang a rack for copper pots and pans. Carry the copper over to the sink; one with a hammered finish will look spectacular. The copper will need a little extra care, so you may want to reserve it for the bar sink and use a more practical porcelain model—preferably a deep one with an exposed apron—for heavy-duty use. Pair that sink with a wall-mounted chrome faucet that has a high-arc spout.

Unfitted cabinetry in the form of a dresser with shelves, a cupboard, or an armoire is quintessential to this style, but you'll probably need storage that is more practical and efficient for contemporary use, too. One way to achieve this is to substitute wall cabinets for open shelves, then use one of the pieces of furniture as an accent and for extra storage. Include wrought-iron hardware in your design, which will coordinate with a wrought-iron chandelier or baker's rack.

Decorate with provincial mini-print fabrics and wallcoverings in mustard yellow, clay red, and the deep blue that is inspired by the lavender that grows all over the region. For authenticity, paint window and door trims blue. Dress windows with lace café curtains and stencil a pretty fleur de lis border around the trim.

Add details, such as flavored oils and vinegars displayed in pretty glass bottles, fresh herbs growing from racks in sunny windows, and blue and white tiles.

smart tip PROVENÇAL STYLE

Keep it simple, and avoid cutesy clutter. A touch of whimsy is fine and always looks at home in a country kitchen, especially when it is handcrafted. One way to achieve a country look is with hardware. Pick up an accent color from the tile or wallpaper, and paint unfinished knobs and pulls, which are available at craft stores. Or mix and match standard metal or glass pieces with a few fun ones. Designs you might consider include fruit, vegetable, or animal motifs.

design workbook

OLD WORLD COUNTRY FLAVORS

earthy accents

To create a kitchen with Old World country charm, use natural materials like rustic wood beams.

baskets on display

Natural woven straw baskets suspended from beams and on the wall add warmth to the kitchen.

freestanding furniture

An antique or reproduction armoire or a chest of drawers creates the right informal and unfitted look.

rustic finishes

Distressed wooden benches and countertop enhance the old country ambiance. (See also top left.)

stone surfaces

A stone wall, left, is the perfect touch for true rustic charm. An arched window completes the picture.

Shaker Style

The basic tenets of the Shaker philosophy, which evolved out of a nineteenth-century religious movement, are built on a sense of humility. "Beauty rests on utility" was their belief. This was reflected in their homes. They believed in using only the most essential elements, completely without ornamentation or frills. Their plain, practical designs featured dovetailed joints and hand-planed tops, plain panels on doors, and legs tapered almost to a pencil point. The finishes on original Shaker cabinets were always dyes and oils, never varnishes, to enhance the wood.

Contemporary cabinet manufacturers, responding to a renewed popularity of the Shaker look during the last decade, have used the Shakers' original designs to inspire similar updated versions of their own. When shopping for Shaker-style cabinetry, look for the same plain paneled doors and wood finishes that are finished to hold up against moisture and grease today. When stained to match the cabinets, a typical Shaker rack of slanted shelves, whether left freestanding or mounted to the wall, makes a great accent piece. Stack a few round, wooden Shaker boxes on the shelves; you can find them in craft stores. Paint them with a color or stain them.

Keeping simplicity in mind, paint the walls in a Shaker-inspired kitchen white. Accent woodwork in colors inspired by natural dyes—terra cotta, yellow ochre, olive green, green-blue, and denim. Ceramic tile installed in a quiltlike pattern on the countertop or backsplash, or as a mural above the cooktop can add more color accents and a reasonable amount of decoration, unless you're a purist at heart. The fixtures should be white or crème-tone with plain fittings in a brushed chrome or pewter finish. Trim kits, available from appliance and cabinet manufacturers, can camouflage the type of modern-day appliances that the Shakers eschewed.

A traditional double-hung window, with or without muntins, fits in fine with the Shaker theme, especially if the trim is kept plain. Install plain wood shutters and panel-style curtains with simple cotton tab tops for an authentic look, or keep the window treatments simple. A tin chandelier and tin wall sconces will pull the look together. Shaker-inspired furniture is widely available today. Tall ladder-back chairs with tape-woven seats look at home around a simple trestle table. A pegged chair rail is a Shaker classic. Installed high on the wall, it can be a display for a collection of handwoven baskets, dried flowers, tapered candles, or even small wooden chairs.

OPPOSITE
The simplicity of Shaker style makes it universally pleasing.

BELOW
The plain-paneled cabinet fronts blend with almost any style.

smart tip SHAKER STYLE

This warm, likable style fits perfectly with a country home because of its old-fashioned look. But it blends well with contemporary interiors, too, because of its clean lines and plain geometric shapes. In fact, a few Shaker elements can warm up the sometimes cold appearance of a contemporary room.

design workbook
A SIMPLE LOOK

form for function

Shaker style cabinets are without extra ornament or trimwork. They are utilitarian yet handsome in their simplicity.

practical design

The center island resembles a Shaker harvest table. The overhang on two sides is for knee room.

traditional seating

The stools are typically Shaker, with their pencil-point legs and rush seats under the padded cushions.

unwasted space

Narrow nooks next to the microwave oven, top left, can be used to hold spices or tall bottles.

pendant lighting

Practical pendant fixtures in a simple design, left, create suitable task and ambient lighting for the kitchen.

Arts and Crafts Style

The Arts and Crafts movement, with roots at the turn of the twentieth century, was a reaction to the ornamentation of Victorian design and the growing use of machines to produce cheap goods. It also professed a philosophy that beautiful, simple, organic objects arranged harmoniously in a house will contribute to one's well-being. The movement's aesthetic is enjoying a resurgence today. Styles that are related to or part of the Arts and Crafts movement include Mission, Craftsman, and Prairie, the signature style of the architect Frank Lloyd Wright.

Start with plain oak cabinets with a handcrafted appearance. As with Shaker style, manufacturers are responding to the public interest in Arts and Crafts, and some offer a line of authentically inspired cabinets. Accessorize with hand-hammered copper hardware. If you can't find genuine examples, shop for reproduc-

tions. The internet is a good place to look for hardware sources. The more wood the better in an Arts and Crafts-style room. Oil the wood well to bring out the grain, and properly seal it against water damage.

For the walls, combine oak wainscoting with a stylized wallpaper—one that combines floral motifs with a geometric pattern; there are wallpaper manufacturers that specialize in this. Select colors that reflect natural hues, such as brown, green, blue, and orange. Accessorize with organically shaped pottery in these colors, too. Pull it all together by incorporating Native American textiles, such as a rug, into this room.

You might want to design a custom-tiled backsplash with matte or "art pottery" glazed tiles. Your lighting design can include a combination of fixtures, such as unobtrusive recessed ceiling canisters and wall lamps with Tiffany-style glass covers or mica shades.

Plain windows should be curtained very simply—if at all—in an Arts and Crafts-style room, using natural fabrics such as linen or muslin with an embroidered border. Typical motifs include ginkgo leaves and poppy seeds. Instead of traditional treatments, use stained glass or art-glass windows: several manufacturers produce an Arts and Crafts line of stained-glass types. To complete the look, furnish the kitchen with a Mission-style table and chairs and a hutch. You may still be able to find authentic pieces at auction.

OPPOSITE
This updated interpretation of the Arts and Crafts style features lighter wood, granite counters, and chrome accents.

LEFT
Light maple cabinets are more cheerful than the dark oak finish typical of authentic Arts and Crafts furniture.

smart tip ARTS AND CRAFTS STYLE

The heart of this style lies in its earthy connection. The more you can bring nature into it, the more authentic it will appear. An easy way to do this is with plants. Open the space up to nature with glass doors that provide a view to a green garden.

design workbook
FAITHFULLY ARTS AND CRAFTS

true to the style

Stained white oak cabinets, slate floors, and reproduction hardware re-create the Arts and Crafts look.

art and nature

The slate mosaic backsplash behind the cook-top depicts a pair of loons. (See also top left.)

furniture inspiration

A built-in buffet, bottom far left, looks remarkably authentic. Note the vintage tele-phone, a nifty accessory.

beverage center

A standalone wine cooler has an art glass door, center left. Refrigerator drawers are underneath it.

fine dining

Just across from the island, a reproduction set of table and chairs, left, pulls the entire room together.

smart steps
the decorating phase

■ Step 1 CREATE A SAMPLE BOARD

Don't make your kitchen decorating all trial and error. Try your ideas out on a sample board first. To make one, use a piece of ½-inch plywood, which is heavy enough to hold your samples but light enough for you to handle. Mount your samples—paint chips, wallpaper swatches, flooring and tile samples, countertop chips, and any other materials you plan to bring into the room—on the board to see how each works as part of the overall scheme. The larger the sample, the better. If a wallpaper pattern clashes with the color or pattern of the tile, or the cabinet color is too bright to match with the floor, change one or both until you find a match that works. The board lets you test your ideas before you start buying materials and risk mistakes that can be costly to fix.

Try different combinations, and look at them in all light levels, night and day. Add photographs of fixtures, appliances, cabinetry, and other items you will include in the room for which you don't have samples to put on the board.

Create a "cheat sheet" to take with you when you shop. (Your full-size sample board is a wonderful resource for building a room that works in harmony, but it will be too awkward to carry with you.) Remembering color shades accurately is nearly impossible. Working without a guide is a sure way to end up with something that doesn't match.

When creating your sample board, include your sources. Note store names for every item, as well as manufacturers and prices. If there are model numbers and color names, record them too. This information will be invaluable if you ever have to touch up or replace an item later. One clever way to keep track of wallpaper style numbers or paint-shade names is to write them on the back of outlet plates.

After completing your project, keep the sample board; it may come in handy if you decide to redecorate the adjoining rooms. With all your samples, it won't be difficult to achieve a cohesive or compatible decorating style in your new kitchen.

Step 2 NOTE THE SIGHT LINES

A sight line is the visual path the eye follows from a given point within a room or from an entrance. A room's primary sight line is the entry. It's the most important one because it draws your attention into the room. Your eye immediately moves in one direction toward whatever is directly opposite the doorway. It may be the range or the door to a backyard garden, but very often in a kitchen it will be the window over the sink. Hopefully, the view is a pleasant one that makes an excellent case for enlarging the window. If possible, install one in a dramatic architectural style. However, if the view is not desirable, an attractive window treatment that is easy to adjust when you want to let in light or close out the outdoors is a good idea. Also, an arrangement of healthy potted plants can help disguise a less-than-perfect view.

LEFT
All of the elements in this kitchen combine to form a cohesive and pleasing decorating style.

ABOVE
Sample of countertop material, tile, and cabinetry were compared before any final purchases were for this design.

If the kitchen entry is located in the middle of the space, the sight line could be a monotonous bank of solid cabinetry, or worse: the dishwasher. Hopefully, this is not the case. The time for relocating major appliances and cabinets is not at the decorating stage; however, if you're still in the planning process and reading this chapter for ideas, review your base map and Chapter Two, "Choose a Layout," beginning on page 30, to see whether you can rearrange things. Remember: a kitchen normally has two or three dominant sight lines, and you have to consider both the sight lines going into the room as well as those going from it.

Inside the kitchen, you may want to situate your table and chairs or snack counter so that when people are seated they don't have to look at the food-preparation area or stare at a wall. Again, if at all possible a view to the outdoors is ideal, but even looking at an attractive collection of pottery artfully arranged in a hutch or a trompe l'oeil window painted on a wall is preferable to facing dirty pots and pans.

Move to other places where you are apt to linger and examine the sight lines. If you entertain in the kitchen, where do guests congregate? At the counter where you set up the buffet? Around the table? If the kitchen is open to other areas of the house, such as the family room, step into those areas and note what you can see when you look into the kitchen. Maybe all you'll have to do is resituate the dining table.

Don't just think about what you don't want to see. Use sight lines to focus attention on attractive elements and to move your eye around the space. Sight lines should be fluid; you don't want the eye to jump from one element to the next. Visual appreciation should flow. The angle of the range hood should draw the eye to the cooktop, for example. The faucet should pull the eye to the sink, then down the counter. The island should make the eye want to travel the length and depth of it before canvassing the outer edges of the room.

Plan your kitchen's sight lines with balance and symmetry in mind. Don't place all of the most powerful visual elements on one side of the room. Find ways to attract attention to all four walls. There should be something interesting to see in all directions but not so much that everything clashes.

Step 3 ADD DETAILS

More than anything else, people react to and remember a room's details—the special touches that take style one step further to a personal level. Details have a powerful effect on the feeling and mood of a room. They usually make the difference between a space that looks professionally designed and one that lacks polish.

Some of the best details are the smallest—exquisite hardware, handsome molding, a stenciled soffit, or a tiled mural, to name a few. Or they could be accessories such as a collection of salt and pepper shakers, antique tins, molds, or other kitchenware, or framed prints grouped on a wall. When creating an arrangement of objects, keep scale and propor-tion in mind. A large object on a small surface looks awkward, a small object on a large surface appears lost. When grouping three or more things, balance one large object with several smaller ones. Keep wall displays at eye level—whether you are standing or sitting. You'll have to adjust them so that they are at a com-fortable height in either position. If a grouping is on the wall behind the table, don't hang it where it can be bumped by someone's head when seated. First, sketch the arrangement to scale on paper, especially if you plan to hang it on the wall. Don't

be afraid to group dissimilar objects. Link them by theme or color. For example, use the same color mat board to coordinate a collection of unrelated framed items. Or paint the frames the same hue.

Step 4 USE COLOR

Color is probably your greatest decorating tool. Don't be afraid of it—it's also one of the easiest things to change. You may want to stick with white or another neutral for permanent fixtures and equipment, although it's possible to change the color of appliances using automotive paint. (Check the Yellow Pages or call an automotive shop to inquire about this service.) But you could opt for color on your cabinets—even as a detail on the molding or on just one section. (See Chapter

Five, "Cabinetry & Storage," beginning on page 100) If the cabinets are wood, you can repaint them later if you want to change the color.

If you are more daring, you could introduce color with your countertop or flooring. Neither of these is necessarily easy or inexpensive to replace if you tire of it, but they aren't major projects, either, especially if they are standard installations of moderately priced materials. However, avoid trendy colors that will date your kitchen; leave most of the color to your walls and accessories.

One of the best ways to test a color is to apply it to a sheet of white poster board, hang it on the wall, and live with it for a few days. Look at it during the day; then wait for evening and look at it again under varying light levels. Does it still appeal to you? What effect does it have on the space at different times of the day? Does it make it appear larger or smaller, warmer or cooler? Do this test for paint, wall-paper, window treatments, tile, and flooring. For an item with a print, find a paint that matches the dominant color, and apply the same test to it.

Color has amazing properties. It can evoke memories, create a mood, or even change your perception of space. Light colors expand a room; dark ones draw the walls in. This is also true of ceilings. If you have a high ceiling that makes your kitchen feel more like a barn, paint the ceiling a deeper shade than the walls to tone down the volume of the space and make the room feel cozier. Visually you are creating an optical illusion that will affect your emotional response to the space, as well.

As a rule of thumb, use no more than three colors in a room. For interest, apply them in varying amounts, shades, and tints. You might want to avoid a mono-chromatic scheme, however, because it tends to become boring. If you are completely set on using one color only, liven it up by adding shading, pattern, and texture. Try a painted finish like ragging, sponging, or glazing.

The stronger the color, the less of it should be used. That's another general rule, which can be broken by personal preference. Remember: a dollop of saturated red equals an entire wall of pale pink in visual interpretation.

When you use two or three colors, combine unequal amounts and different shades of each, along with a dash of black, white, or another neutral. If you don't do this, your eyes won't know where to focus. Let one color dominate. Anchor accent colors in opposite parts of the room. For example, you can pick up one color from the wallpaper in the curtains, then use the same color for the cushions on chairs or stools.

Where do you get your color inspiration? For an explosion of color, visit the produce aisle of a grocery store or the local garden nursery. Comb through fashion magazines and art books. Look inside your clothes closet. Tear out pictures of anything with color that attracts you. Keep a record in your design notebook. After you've got a stack of tearsheets, separate them by color. Undoubtedly a pattern will emerge. Whatever color dominates that collection is a good indicator of what pleases you most of the time.

Wallpaper, Paint, and Fabric

While thinking about color for the kitchen, also consider the type of paint, wallpaper, and fabric to use. Anything that isn't wash-able should be out of the question. Dust and grime cling to the grease that accumulates in a kitchen—no matter how much vent-ing you install and how meticulous you are about wiping up spills. And germs thrive around moisture—not just at the sink but at the cooktop, too. Just look at the wet wall behind your range the next time you steam vegetables.

Luckily, it isn't difficult to find materials and products that are designed to hold up better and clean more easily than ever before. Some paints, wallpapers, wallpaper glues, and fabrics also contain a mildewcide, which may be an advantage if your kitchen doesn't get enough ventilation.

After you've chosen a color scheme, look for wallpaper and fabrics to carry your theme through. You can also use wallpaper to suggest a theme or decorative style in the kitchen. Many man-ufacturers have produced new designs that reinterpret historical motifs, for example. Use them, later, to pick up a solid color for accents, wall color, or trim.

OPPOSITE TOP
A golden-yellow paint color brings out the warmth in the wood cabinetry.

OPPOSITE BOTTOM
A chic French country pattern was used to upholster a banquet and side chairs in this eat-in kitchen. Coordi-nating table linens make the setting even more inviting.

Before doing anything, review the sight lines from outside the room and any adjoining spaces, especially any areas you must pass through to get to the kitchen. Think of them sequentially. Ideally, there should be an interrelationship among all the patterns and colors that run from room to room. If you want stripes in the kitchen but an adjoining area has a floral print, match the colors.

In a small kitchen, as a rule, a bold print may be too busy. On the other hand, it may be just what's needed to make a large space cozier. Vertical designs will make the ceiling appear higher and tailored; horizon-tal patterns will move your eye from one corner to the next; random pat-terns are informal in feeling. In gen-eral, traditional rooms look best with patterned wallpaper, especially if there is trimwork. In contemporary settings, let the architecture and materials speak for themselves.

9

remodeling timeline

There are many variables that can affect the pace and timing of your project. If you're doing any of the work yourself, you may be able to estimate how much time you'll spend judging by previous experience with similar jobs. Remember, depending on local codes, there are some jobs for which you may have to hire a licensed professional. Whether you hire out some or all of the work, every contractor works differently, and each job may present its own glitches. However, there are steps that divide up the process into logical sequences that eventually result in a finished design. On the next two pages is a timeline of events that will help you gauge the work that is involved, in a sequential fashion. The time lengths indicated for the stages are approximate for an average-size kitchen project using standard products and materials.

Certain aspects of your project may add to the timeframe. Semi-custom cabinets like these can take up to a few months to be ready.

smart steps
project scheduling

■ ### Step 1 PREPLANNING
- ■ Make the decision to remodel.
- ■ Assess the problems and goals involved.
- ■ Gather ideas, and review trends.
- ■ Develop a budget, and obtain financing.
- ■ Collect information about contractors.
- ■ Arrange interviews with contractors.
- ■ Select a contractor.

■ ### Step 3 DESIGN AND AGREEMENT
- ■ Meet with the designer for presentation of preliminary drawings and project specifications.
- ■ Review and discuss options.
- ■ Sign a design agreement.

4 WEEKS	1 WEEK	2-3 WEEKS	2-4 WEEKS

■ ### Step 2 INITIAL MEETINGS
- ■ Walk through the existing space.
- ■ Brainstorm with the contractor.
- ■ Decide whether the project is feasible within the budget.
- ■ Sign a letter of intent if you're purchasing design services, or skip to step 4.

■ ### Step 4 DESIGN DEVELOPMENT
- ■ Review completed drawings and project notes.
- ■ Clarify any misunderstandings about the scope and intent of the project.
- ■ Select products.
- ■ Sign the construction contract.
- ■ Make the first down payment.
- ■ Wait three days for the Right of Recision period to pass, if applicable.
- ■ Obtain permits.
- ■ Meet with the construction team, and sign a preconstruction agreement.

Step 5 AFTER PERMITS ARE ISSUED

- Order products.
- Finalize the project schedule, and distribute it.
- Discuss impact of project on home life with the family, including safety and keeping pets out of the workplace.
- Remove personal items and breakables from the construction area.

Step 7 FINAL STAGES

- Inspect the job, and establish a list of final details to make sure everything is completed to your satisfaction.
- Obtain the final inspection and certificate of occupancy or habitability.
- Make a substantial completion payment.

| 1 WEEK | 4-8 WEEKS | 1 WEEK | 1 WEEK |

Step 6 THE WORK

- Complete the demolition.
- Complete the framing.
- Rough-in mechanical systems.
- Install the drywall.
- Install the flooring.
- Install the cabinetry.
- Install fixtures.
- Do the finishing work (painting and wallpapering).

Step 8 THE CONCLUSION

- Give the final approval.
- Make the final payment.

appendix KITCHEN TEMPLATES

Cabinets

Row 1: 6"x24", 6"x24", 6"x24", 6"x24", 6"x24", 6"x24", desk 36"x24", desk 30"x24", 9"x24", 9"x24", 9"x24", 9"x24", 9"x24", 9"x24", 9"x24", 9"x24"

Row 2: 12"x24", 12"x24", 12"x24", 12"x24", 12"x24", 12"x24", 12"x24", 6"x24", base cabinet 15"x24", base cabinet 15"x24", base cabinet 15"x24", base cabinet 15"x24", base cabinet 15"x24", base cabinet 15"x24", base cabinet 15"x24", base cabinet 15"x24"

Row 3: base cabinet 15"x24", 9"x24", 6"x24", base cabinet 18"x24", base cabinet 18"x24", base cabinet 18"x24", base cabinet 18"x24", base cabinet 18"x24", base cabinet 18"x24", base cabinet 18"x24", base cabinet 18"x24", base cabinet 18"x24", base cabinet 18"x24", base cabinet 18"x24"

Row 4: base cabinet 21"x24", base cabinet 21"x24", base cabinet 21"x24", base cabinet 21"x24", base cabinet 21"x24", base cabinet 21"x24", 9"x24", base cabinet 24"x24", base cabinet 24"x24", base cabinet 24"x24", base cabinet 24"x24", base cabinet 24"x24"

Row 5: base cabinet 24"x24", base cabinet 24"x24", base cabinet 24"x24", base cabinet 24"x24", base cabinet 24"x24", 9"x24", base cabinet 27"x24", base cabinet 27"x24", base cabinet 27"x24", base cabinet 27"x24", base cabinet 27"x24"

Row 6: base cabinet 27"x24", base cabinet 15"x24", base cabinet 30"x24", base cabinet 30"x24", base cabinet 30"x24", base cabinet 30"x24", base cabinet 30"x24", base cabinet 30"x24", base cabinet 30"x24", base cabinet 30"x24"

Row 7: base cabinet 33"x24", base cabinet 33"x24", base cabinet 33"x24", base cabinet 33"x24", base cabinet 33"x24", 12"x24", base cabinet 36"x24", base cabinet 36"x24", base cabinet 36"x24"

Row 8: base cabinet 36"x24", base cabinet 36"x24", base cabinet 36"x24", base cabinet 36"x24", base cabinet 36"x24", base cabinet 36"x24", base cabinet 39"x24", base cabinet 39"x24"

Row 9: base cabinet 39"x24", base cabinet 39"x24", base cabinet 39"x24", base cabinet 42"x24", base cabinet 42"x24", base cabinet 42"x24", base cabinet 18"x24", base cabinet 18"x24"

Row 10: base cabinet 42"x24", base cabinet 45"x24", base cabinet 45"x24", base cabinet 45"x24", base cabinet 45"x24", base cabinet 45"x24", base cabinet 45"x24"

Row 11: base cabinet 45"x24", left-hand corner-base cabinet 36"x24", left-hand corner-base cabinet 36"x24", left-hand corner-base cabinet 36"x24", right-hand corner-base cabinet 36"x24", right-hand corner-base cabinet 36"x24", right-hand corner-base cabinet 36"x24", right-hand corner-base cabinet 36"x24"

Pantry Cabinets

pantry 18"x12" · pantry 24"x12" · pantry 24"x12" · pantry 36"x12" · pantry 24"x18" · pantry 24"x18" · pantry 24"x24" · pantry 24"x24" · pantry 36"x24"

Islands and Appliances

washer 26"x27" · dryer 29"x27" · stack washer dryer 25"x27" · compact washer 24"x24" · compact dryer 24"x24" · island 24"x24" · island 36"x24" · island 36"x24"

island 60"x"30 · island 30"x36" · island 40"x36" · island 48"x36" · 36" · 36" · 24" · 24"

refrigerator 30"x29" · refrigerator 33"x29" · refrigerator 36"x29" · refrigerator 24"x24" · refrigerator 42"x24" · refrigerator 60"x24" · refrigerator 24"x24" · refrigerator 18"x24"

range 20"x24" · range 24"x24" · range 30"x24" · range 36"x24" · range 48"x24" · cooktop 30"x21" · cooktop 36"x21" · cooktop 48"x21"

grill 21"x24" · hood 24" · hood 30" · hood 36" · hood 48" · wall oven 24"x24" · wall oven 27"x24" · microwave 30"x18" · microwave 22"x18"

microwave 22"x18" · trash compactor 15"x24" · dishwasher 24"x24"

Sinks

sink 24"x22" · sink 33"x22" · sink 36"x22" · sink 38"x22" · sink 42"x22" · sink 42"x22"

sink 43"x22" · sink 48"x22" · sink 60"x22" · sink 22" · sink 22"x22" · bar sink 15"x22"

Countertops

Tables

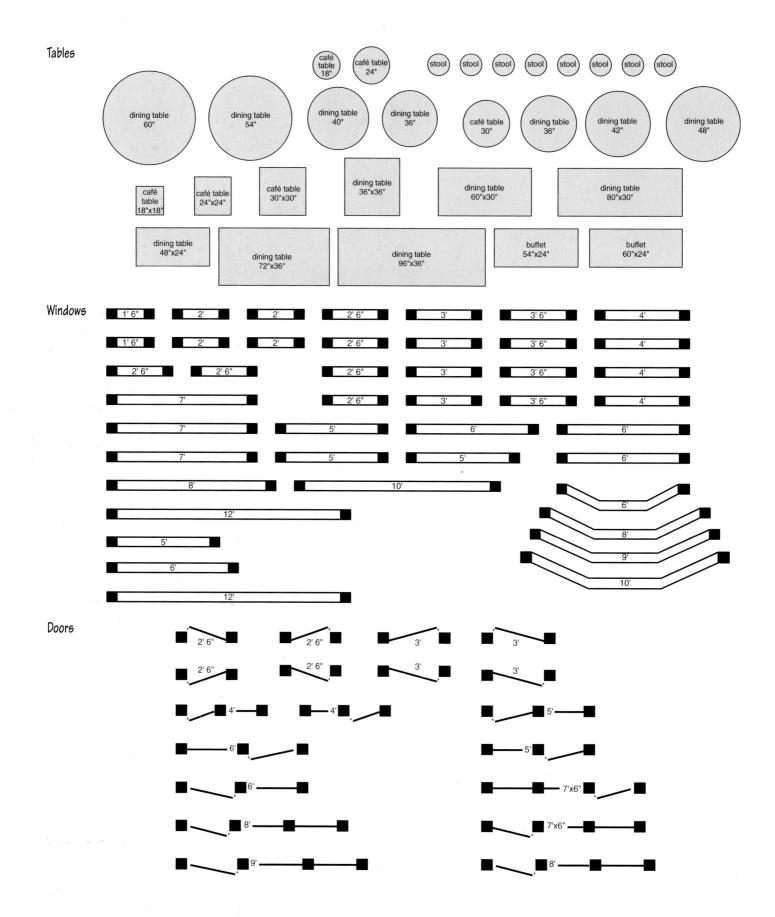

Windows

Doors

Scale: 1 square=1 foot

resource guide

The following list of manufacturers and associations is meant to be a general guide to additional industry and product-related sources. It is not intended as a listing of products and manufacturers represented by the photographs in this book.

Above View
4750 S. 10th St.
Milwaukee, WI 53221
Phone: 414-744-7118
www.aboveview.com
Makes ornamental ceiling tiles

Adagio, Inc.
6353 W. Rogers Circle
Boca Raton, FL 33487
www.adagiosinks.com
Phone: 877-988-2297
Makes hand-crafted sinks in a variety of materials

Amana
403 W. 4th St.
Newton, IA 50208
Phone: 800-843-0304
www.amana.com
Manufactures refrigerators, dishwashers, and cooking appliances.

American Olean Tile Co.
1000 Cannon Ave.
Lansdale, PA 19446-0271
Phone: 215-855-1111
www.americanolean.com
Manufactures ceramic tile.

American Standard
1 Centennial Plaza, P. O. Box 6820
Piscataway, NJ 08855-6820
www.americanstandard-us.com
Manufactures plumbing and tile products.

Andersen
100 4th Ave. North
Bayport, MN 55003-1096
Phone: 888-888-7020
www.andersencorp.com
Manufactures an extensive range of window and skylight styles; also carries a selection of patio doors

Ann Sacks Tile and Stone, part of the Kohler Company
1210 SE Grand Ave.
Portland, OR 97214
Phone: 800-278-8453
www.annsacks.com
Manufactures a broad line of tile and stone, including terra-cotta and mosaics

Armstrong World Industries
2500 Columbia Ave.
P.O. Box 3001
Lancaster, PA 17604
Phone: 800-233-3823
www.armstrong.com
Manufactures floors, cabinets, and ceilings for both home and commercial use. Its Web site features a design showcase for consumer reference

Artemide
1980 New Highway
Farmingdale NY 11735
Phone: 631-694 9292
www.artemide.com
Manufactures lighting fixtures

Bach Faucets
19701 DaVinci
Lake Forest, CA 92610
Phone: 866-863-6584
www.bachfaucet.com
Manufactures faucets

Benjamin Moore & Co.
51 Chestnut Ridge Rd.
Montvale, NJ 07645
www.benjaminmoore.com
Manufactures paint

Big Chill Refrigerators
Phone: 877-842-3269
www.bigchillfridge.com
Manufactures retro-style refrigerators

Blanco America
110 Mount Holly By-Pass
Lumberton, NJ 08048
www.blancoamerica.com
Manufactures sinks and faucets

Bosch Home Appliances
5551 McFadden Ave.
Huntington Beach, CA 92807
Phone: 714-901-6600
www.boschappliances.com
Manufactures major and small appliances

Brewster Wallcovering Co.
67 Pacella Park Dr.
Randolph, MA 02368
Phone: 781-963-4800
www.brewsterwallcovering.com
Manufactures wallpaper, fabrics, and borders in many patterns and styles

Bruce Hardwood Floors, Div. of Armstrong World Industries
P.O. Box 3001
Lancaster, PA 17604
Phone: 800-233-3823
www.bruce.com
Manufactures hardwood flooring

Corian, Div. of DuPont
Chestnut Run Plaza
721 Maple Run
P.O. Box 80721
Wilmington, DE 19880
Phone: 800-426-7426
www.corian.com
Manufactures solid-surfacing material for home and commercial kitchens

Country Curtains
At The Red Lion Inn
P. O. Box 955
Stockbridge, MA 01262
Phone: 800-456-0321
www.countrycurtains.com
A national retailer and on-line source for ready-made curtains, draperies, shades, blinds, hardware, and accessories

Crossville, Inc.
P.O. Box 1168
Crossville, TN 38557
Phone: 931-484-2110
www.crossvilleinc.com
Manufactures porcelain, stone, and metal tile

Delta Faucet Co.
55 E. 111th St.
P.O. Box 40980
Indianapolis, IN 46280
Phone: 317-848-1812
www.deltafaucet.com
Manufactures a variety of faucets and finishes for kitchen and bath

Dex Studios
Phone: 404-753-0600
www.dexstudios.com
Creates custom concrete sinks and countertops

Elkay
2222 Camden Ct.
Oak Brook, IL 60523
Phone: 630-574-8484
www.elkayusa.com
Manufactures sinks, faucets, and countertops

Eisenhart Wallcoverings Co.
400 Pine St.
Hanover, PA 17331
Phone: 800-555-2554
www.eisenhartwallcoverings.com
Manufactures wallpaper and borders for the home

Fisher and Paykel
5900 Skylab Rd.
Huntington Beach, CA 92647
Phone: 888-936-7872
www.fisherandpaykel.com
Manufactures kitchen appliances

Florida Tile
P. O. Box 447
Lakeland, FL 33802
Phone: 800-242-9042
www.floridatile.com
Distributor and manufacturer of ceramic wall and floor tile

Formica Corporation
225 E. 5th St.
Ste. 200
Cincinnati, OH 45202
Phone: 800-367-6422
www.formica.com
Manufactures plastic laminate and solid-surfacing material

Frigidaire
P.O. Box 212378
Martinez, GA 30917
Phone: 800-374-4432
www.frigidaire.com
Manufacturers major appliances, including ranges, cooktops, refrigerators, and dishwashers

General Electric
GE Customer Relations
P.O. Box 22108
Memphis, TN 38122
Phone: 800-626-2000
www.geappliances.com
Manufactures refrigerators, dishwashers, ovens, and other major appliances

Glidden
Phone: 800-454-3336
www.glidden.com
Manufactures paint

Green Mountain Soapstone Corp.
680 E. Hubbardton Rd.
P.O. Box 807
Castleton, VT 05735
Phone: 802-468-5636
www.greenmountainsoapstone.com
Manufactures soapstone floors, walls, sinks, and countertops

Haier America
Phone: 877-337-3639
www.haieramerica.com
Manufactures electronics and appliances, including wine cellars

Hartco, a div. of Armstrong World Industries
www.hartco.com
Manufactures hardwood flooring

Italian Trade Commission
Ceramic Tile Dept.
33 E. 67th St.
New York, NY 10021
Phone: 212-980-1500
www.italytile.com
An organization that promotes Italian tile, offering consumers a guide to buying Italian ceramic tile

Jenn-Air, a part of the Maytag Corporation
Maytag Customer Service
240 Edwards St.
Cleveland, TN 37311
Phone: 800-688-1100
www.jennair.com
Manufactures major kitchen appliances including cooktops, ranges, and ovens

Kemiko Concrete Products
P.O. Box 1109
Leonard, TX 75452-3677
Phone: 903-587-3708
www.kemiko.com
Manufactures acid stains for concrete flooring and other concrete products; creates decorative concrete floors

Kohler
444 Highland Dr.
Kohler, WI 53044
Phone: 800-456-4537
www.kohlerco.com
Manufactures kitchen and bath sinks, faucets, and related accessories that include hot-water, soap, and lotion dispensers, as well as colanders, drainboards, and wire-rinse baskets

KraftMaid Cabinetry
P.O. Box 1055
Middlefield, OH 44062
Phone: 888-562-7744
www.kraftmaid.com
Manufactures stock and built-to-order cabinets with a variety of finishes and storage options

LG
1000 Sylvan Ave.
Englewood Cliffs, NJ 07632
Phone: 800-243-0000
www.lge.com
Manufactures major appliances

Lightology
1718 W. Fullerton Ave.
Chicago, IL 60614
866-954-4489
www.lightology.com
Manufactures lighting fixtures

Maytag Corp.
240 Edwards St.
Cleveland, TN 37311
Phone: 800-688-9900
www.maytag.com
Manufactures major appliances

Merillat Industries
5353 W. U.S. 223
P.O. Box 1946
Adrian, MI 49221
Phone: 800-575-8763
www.merillat.com
Manufactures kitchen and bath cabinetry

MGS Progetti
C.so Milano, 189
28883 Gravellona Toce
(VB) - Italy
www.mgsprogetti.com
Manufactures faucets

Miele
9 Independence Way
Princeton, NJ 08540
Phone: 800-843-7231
www.miele.com
Manufactures major appliances

Moen
25300 Al Moen Dr.
North Olmsted, OH 44070
Phone: 800-289-6636
www.moen.com
*Manufactures faucets, sinks, and accessories for both
kitchen and bath*

National Association of Remodeling Industry (NARI)
780 Lee St., Ste. 200
Des Plaines, IL 60016
Phone: 800-611-6274
www.nari.org
*A professional organization for remodelers, contractors,
and design/remodelers; also offers consumer information*

National Kitchen and Bath Association (NKBA)
687 Willow Grove St.
Hackettstown, NJ 07840
Phone: 800-843-6522
www.nkba.org
*A national trade organization for kitchen and bath design
professionals; offers consumers product information
and a referral service*

Native Trails
Phone: 800-786-0862
www.nativetrails.net
A source for handcrafted copper sinks and Talavera tiles

Plain and Fancy Custom Cabinetry
Oak St. and Rte. 501
Schaeffertown, PA 17088
Phone: 800-447-9006
www.plainfancycabinetry.com
Makes custom cabinetry

Price Pfister, Inc.
19701 Da Vinci
Foothill Ranch, CA 92610
Phone: 800-732-8238
www.pricepfister.com
Manufactures faucets

Robbins, Div. of Armstrong World Industries
P.O. Box 3001
Lancaster, PA 17604
Phone: 800-233-3823
www.robbins.com
Makes hardwood flooring

Rocky Mountain Hardware
P.O. Box 4108
1030 Airport Way
Hailey, ID 83333
Phone: 888-788-2013
www.rockymountainhardware.com
*Offers hardware accessories for the home including kitchen,
bath, and window hardware*

Seagull Lighting Products, Inc.
301 W. Washington St.
Riverside, NJ 08075
856-764-0500
www.seagulllighting.com
Manufactures lighting fixtures

Sharp USA
Sharp Plaza
Mahwah, NJ 07430
Phone: 800-237-4277
www.sharpusa.com
*Manufactures electronics and small appliances, including
microwaves, air conditioners, and high-speed ovens*

Sherwin-Williams
www.sherwinwilliams.com
Manufactures paint

Sonoma Cast Stone
P.O. Box 1721
Sonoma, CA 95476
Phone: 888-807-4234
www.sonomastone.com
Designs and builds concrete sinks and countertops

Sub-Zero
P.O. Box 44130
Madison, WI 53744-4130
Phone: 800-222-7820
www.subzero.com
Manufactures refrigerators and freezers in full sizes and as modular drawer-style units

Tile Council Of America
100 Clemson Research Blvd.
Anderson, SC 29625
Phone: 864-646-8453
www.tileusa.com
A trade organization dedicated to promoting the tile industry; also provides consumer information on selecting and installing tile

Thibaut Inc.
480 Frelinghuysen Ave.
Newark, NJ 07114
Phone: 800-223-0704
www.thibautdesign.com
Manufactures wallpaper and fabrics

Viking Range Corp.
111 Front St.
Greenwood, MS 38930
Phone: 888-845-4641
www.vikingrange.com
Manufactures professional-style kitchen appliances

Wilsonart International
P.O. Box 6110
Temple, TX 76503-6110
Phone: 800-433-3222
www.wilsonart.com
Manufactures solid-surfacing materials, plastic laminates, and adhesive for kitchen countertops, cabinets, floors, and fixtures

Wolf Appliance Company, Div. of Sub-Zero
P.O. Box 44848
Madison, WI 53744
Phone: 800-222-7820
www.wolfappliance.com
Manufactures professional-style ranges, cooktops, and other appliances

York Wallcoverings
750 Linden Ave.
York, PA 17405
Phone: 800-375-9675
www.yorkwall.com
Sells a wide variety of wallpapers and borders; offers on-line decorating tips and advice

glossary OF KITCHEN TERMS

Absorption (light): The light energy (wavelengths) not reflected by an object or substance. The color of a substance depends on the wavelength reflected.

Accent light: A type of light that highlights an area to emphasize that aspect of a room's character.

Accessible designs: Those that accommodate persons with physical disabilities.

Adaptable designs: Those that can be easily changed to accommodate a person with disabilities.

Ambient light: General light that surrounds a room and is not focused.

Antiscalding valve (pressure-balancing valve): A fitting that contains a piston that automatically responds to changes in line water pressure to maintain temperature; the valve blocks abrupt drops or rises in temperature.

Awning window: A window that is hinged at the top and swings outward when open.

Backlighting: Illumination coming from a source behind or at the side of an object.

Backsplash: The vertical part at the rear and sides of a countertop that protects the adjacent wall.

Barrier-free fixture: A fixture specifically designed to allow access to people who use wheelchairs or who have limited mobility.

Base cabinet: A cabinet that rests on the floor and supports a countertop.

Base plan: A map of the existing kitchen that shows detailed measurements and the location of cabinets, appliances, sinks, and any fixed elements.

Basin: A shallow sink.

Bump out: Living space created by cantilevering the floor and ceiling joists and extending the exterior wall of a room.

Butcher block: A countertop material composed of strips of hardwood laminated together and sealed against moisture penetration.

Candlepower (Cp): The intensity of light measured at a lamp. This term is generally used for task and accent lighting.

Cantilever: A structural beam supported on one end. A cantilever can be used to support a small addition.

Casement window: A window that consists of one or two framed-glass panels that are hinged on the side and swing outward at the turn of a crank.

Centerline: The bisecting line through the center of an object, such as a sink.

CFM: An abbreviation that refers to cubic feet of air that is moved per minute by an exhaust fan.

Clearance: The space between two fixtures, the centerlines of two fixtures, or a fixture and an obstacle, such as a wall. Clearances may be mandated by codes.

Code: A locally or nationally enforced mandate regarding structural design, materials, plumbing, or electrical systems that state what you can or cannot do when you build or remodel. Codes are intended to protect standards of health, safety, and land use.

Color intensity: Strength of a color.

Color rendition index (CRI): Measures the way a light source renders color. The higher the number, the more the color resembles how it appears in sunlight.

Contemporary style: A style of decoration or architecture that is modern and pertains to what is current.

Correlated color temperature (CCT): Compares the apparent warmth or coolness of discontinuous-spectrum light.

Dimmer Switch: A switch that can vary the intensity of the light source that it controls.

Downlighting: A lighting technique that illuminates objects or areas from above.

Double-hung window: A window that consists of two framed-glass panels that slide open vertically, guided by a metal or wood track.

Fittings: The plumbing devices that bring water to the fixtures. These can include faucets, spouts, and drains, etc.

Fixed window: A window that cannot be opened. It is usually a decorative unit, such as a half-round or Palladian-style window.

Fixture: Any fixed part of the structural design, such as sinks, windows, or doors.

Fixture spacing: Refers to how far apart to space ambient-light fixtures for an even field of light.

Fluorescent light bulb: An energy-efficient light source made of a usually tubular-shaped bulb that contains a glowing gas and is coated on the inside with phosporous.

Foot-candle (Fc): A unit used to measure the brightness produced by a lamp. A foot-candle is equal to one lumen per square foot of surface.

Framed cabinet: A cabinet with a full frame across the face of the cabinet box.

Frameless cabinet: A cabinet without a face frame. It may also be called a "European-style" cabinet.

Ground-fault circuit interrupter (GFCI): A safety circuit breaker that compares the amount of current entering a receptacle with the amount leaving. If there is a discrepancy of 0.005 volt, the GFCI breaks the circuit in a fraction of a second. GFCIs are required by the National Electrical Code in areas of the house that are subject to dampness.

Grout: A binder and filler applied to the joints between ceramic tile.

Halogen light bulb: A bulb that uses metal halides to provide incandescent light that is whiter and brighter than standard incandescent lamps.

Hardware: Wood, metal, or plastic trim found on the exterior of furniture or cabinetry, such as knobs, handles, and decorative trim.

Highlight: The lightest tone in a room.

Incandescent light: A bulb that contains a conductive wire filament through which current flows. This is the most common type of light source.

Load-bearing wall: A wall that supports part of a structure's weight.

Lumen: A term that refers to the intensity of light measured at a light source that is used for general or ambient lighting.

Muntins: Framing members of a window that divide the panes of glass.

Palette: A range of colors that complement each other in a scheme.

Peninsula: A countertop, with or without a base cabinet, that is connected at one end to a wall or another counter and extends outward, providing access on three sides.

Pressure-balancing valve: See "Antiscalding Valve."

Recessed light fixtures: Light fixtures that are installed into ceilings, soffits, or cabinets and are flush with the surrounding area.

Reflectance levels: The amount of light that is reflected from a colored surface, such as a tile wall or painted surface.

Roof window: A window that is installed on the roof and can be opened to provide ventilation.

Schematic: A detailed diagram of systems (such as plumbing or electrical) within a home.

Sight line: The natural line of sight that the eye travels when looking into or around a room. Objects can be arranged to create a more aesthetic sight line.

Skylight: A framed opening in the roof that admits sunlight into the house. It can be covered with either a flat glass panel or plastic dome, and in some cases can be openable.

Snap-in grilles: Ready-made and easy to install rectangular or diamond-pattern grilles that snap into a window sash and create the look of a true divided-light window.

Soffit: The area just below the ceiling and above the wall cabinets. It may be boxed in or open.

Space reconfiguration: A term used to describe the reallocation of interior space without adding on.

Spout: The projecting tube-like orifice from which water flows out of a faucet.

Subfloor: The material applied directly to the floor joists on top of which the finished floor rests.

Task lighting: Lighting designed to illuminate a particular task area; especially useful in high-work areas.

Tone: Degree of lightness or darkness of a color.

Universal design: Products and room designs that are easy to use by people of all ages and varying abilities.

Wall cabinet: A cabinet, usually 12 inches deep, that's mounted on the wall a minimum of 12 inches above a countertop.

Work triangle: The area bounded by the lines that connect the sink, range, and refrigerator.

index

photo credits

page 1: Anne Gummerson, architect: Laura Thomas, Melville-Thomas Architects **page 2:** Beth Singer, design/build: Millenium Cabinets, design: Kevin McManamon Interiors **page 6:** Mark Samu **page 8:** Ken Gutmaker **page 10:** Eric Roth, design: Dahlia Kitchen Design **pages 12–13:** both Eric Roth, design: Dahlia Kitchen Design **page 14:** Eric Roth, architect: David Stirling, Stirling Brown Architects **page 15:** James Chen **page 16:** Jessie Walker **page 19:** Anne Gummerson, architect: Hammond-Wilson Architects **pages 20–21:** both Tria Giovan **pages 22–23:** davidduncanlivingston.com **page 24:** both Eric Roth **pages 26–29:** all Mark Samu **page 30:** Anne Gummerson, architect: Brian Swanson **pages 32–34:** all Bob Greenspan, stylist: Susan Andrews **page 35:** Jessie Walker, design: Linda Brown **pages 36–38:** all Bob Greenspan, stylist: Susan Andrews **page 41:** Eric Roth **page 45:** Jessie Walker **pages 50–51:** all Mark Samu, design: Rita Grants **pages 52–55:** all Mark Samu **pages 56–57:** melabee m miller, architect: Studio Tagland **pages 58–59:** Mark Samu **page 60:** davidduncanlivingston.com **page 62:** Beth Singer, design: Braam's Design **pages 63–64:** all davidduncanlivingston.com **page 65:** top davidduncanlivingston.com; bottom Jessie Walker, design: Gail Drury, Drury Design **page 66:** davidduncanlivingston.com **page 67:** both Jessie Walker, design: David T. Smith, The Workshops of David T. Smith **pages 69–71:** all davidduncanlivingston.com **page 72:** Anne Gummerson, architect: Sara Schweizer **pages 74–81:** all davidduncanlivingston.com **page 82:** top davidduncanlivingston.com; bottom Tria Giovan **pages 83–84:** both davidduncanlivingston.com **page 85:** courtesy of Armstrong **page 86:** Tria Giovan **page 87:** Mark Lohman, design: Cheryl Hamilton-Gray **page 88:** Anne Gummerson, design: Kelly Dodd, builder: Kenwood Kitchens **page 89:** top Mark Lohman; bottom davidduncanlivingston.com **page 90:** davidduncanlivingston.com **page 91:** Mark Samu, design: Lucianna Samu **page 92:** Anne Gummerson, design/builder: Gilday Design-Build **pages 93–97:** all davidduncanlivingston.com **pages 98–99:** all Tria Giovan **page 100:** Anne Gummerson, design: Gina Fitzsimmons, Fitzsimmons Design Associates **page 102:** courtesy of Kraftmaid **page 103:** left Jessie Walker, design: Gail Drury, Drury Design; right Tony Giammarino/Giammarino & Dworkin, design: Madrone Custom Cabinets **page 104:** bottom right Mark Lohman, design: Roxanne Packham Design & Michele Hughes Design; bottom left & top left Anne Gummerson **page 105:** top Jessie Walker, design: Gail Drury, Drury Design; bottom Tria Giovan **page 106:** Tria Giovan **page 107:** top right Anne Gummerson, design: Gina Fitzsimmons, Fitzsimmons Design Associates; bottom Anne Gummerson, design: Snaidero Kitchens; top left davidduncanlivingston.com **page 108:** Tria Giovan **page 109:** Mark Lohman, design: Janet Lohman Interior Design **page 110:** Tria Giovan **page 111:** top Minh + Wass, design: Lorcan O'Herlihy; bottom Tria Giovan **page 112:** top Jessie Walker, design: David T. Smith, The Workshops of David T. Smith; bottom left Jessie Walker, design: Neff Kitchen Design; bottom right Tony Giammarino/ Giammarino & Dworkin, design: K. Kowach **page 113:** Beth Singer, design/retail: Kitchen Studio, design: Austerberry Interiors **page 114:** all Eric Roth, design: Dahlia Kitchen Design **page 115:** Mark Lohman, architect: Burdge & Associates **page 116:** Beth Singer, cabinets & appliances: Trevarrow Inc., design: Pam Bytner Design **page 118:** Mark Lohman, architect: Burdge & Associates **page 119:** both Tony Giammarino/Giammarino & Dworkin, design: Madrone Custom Cabinets **page 120:** Mark Lohman, design: Carol Hanes, Shamrock Design **page 121:** Jessie Walker, design: Gail Drury, Drury Design **pages 122–123:** courtesy of Wolf **page 124:** davidduncanlivingston.com **page 125:** courtesy of GE **page 126:** Beth Singer, design/retail: Kitchen Studio **page 127:** Mark Lohman, design: Cynthia Marks Interior Design **page 128:**

Mark Lohman, design: Cheryl Hamilton-Gray **page 129:** Bob Greenspan, stylist: Susan Andrews **page 130:** Beth Singer, design/build: Lafata Cabinets **page 131:** left courtesy of Wolf; right courtesy of Kraftmaid **page 132:** top Mark Samu, design: Jean Stoffer; bottom Mark Lohman, design: Lynn Pries Design **page 133:** Mark Lohman **page 134:** Bob Greenspan, stylist: Susan Andrews **page 135:** Beth Singer, cabinets & appliances: Trevarrow Inc., design: Pam Bytner Design **page 136:** Beth Singer, design/retail: Kitchen Studio, design: Kevin McManamon Interiors **page 137:** top Mark Samu, design: Courland Design; bottom Mark Lohman **page 138:** both courtesy of Sub-Zero **page 139:** Mark Lohman, design: Sally Dixon Design **page 140:** left courtesy of GE; right courtesy of Fisher & Paykel **page 141:** Bob Greenspan, stylist: Susan Andrews **page 142:** courtesy of Moen **page 143:** top Bob Greenspan, stylist: Susan Andrews; bottom Mark Lohman **page 144:** Mark Lohman, design: Will McGaul & Co. **page 147:** Joseph DeLeo **page 149:** Beth Singer, design/retail: Kitchen Studio **page 150:** Bob Greenspan, stylist: Susan Andrews **page 151:** Beth Singer, design/build: Kitchen Studio **pages 152–153:** all Beth Singer, cabinets & appliances: Trevarrow Inc., design/retail: DeGiulio Kitchen and Bath **page 155:** Tria Giovan **page 156:** Mark Lohman, design: Susan

Cohen Design **page 157:** Beth Singer, design: Kitchens by Diane, architect: Robert Summers, builder: B&B Investments **page 158:** Mark Lohman, design: Dana Jones, The Kitchen Consultant **page 159:** Jessie Walker, architect: Lenore Bagelman, Full Circle Architects **page 160:** Mark Lohman, design: Marlene Rice **page 162:** Mark Lohman **page 163:** top Mark Lohman; bottom Nancy Elizabeth Hill **pages 164–165:** top right Mark Lohman; bottom right davidduncanlivingston.com; bottom left Tony Giammarino/Giammarino & Dworkin; top left Mark Lohman, design: Sally Dixon Design **page 166:** Tria Giovan **pages 168–169:** both davidduncanlivingston.com **pages 170–171:** both Bob Greenspan, stylist: Susan Andrews **pages 172–173:** all Anne Gummerson, design: Gina Fitzsimmons, Fitzsimmons Design Associates **pages 174–175:** both davidduncanlivingston.com **pages 176–177:** all Jessie Walker, design: David Hagerman **pages 178–179:** both davidduncanlivingston.com **pages 180–181:** all Mark Lohman, design: Debbie Jones **page 182:** davidduncanlivingston.com **page 183:** Mark Lohman, design: Kyser Interiors **pages 184–185:** all davidduncanlivingston.com **pages 186–187:** both Jessie Walker, design: Cynthia Muni **pages 188–189:** Todd Caverly **pages 190–191:** both Jessie Walker, design: Gail Drury, Drury Design **page 192:** all Jessie Walker,

design: Jim & Jean Wagner, Woodfellows **page 193:** Jessie Walker **pages 194–195:** center Anne Gummerson, design: David Mitchell; right Anne Gummerson **pages 196–197:** both Mark Lohman, design: Janet Lohman Interior Design **page 198:** both Mark Lohman, design: Kyser Interiors **page 200:** Phillip H. Ennis Photography, design: John Buscarello **page 202:** all Phillip H. Ennis Photography, design: John Buscarello **page 203:** all davidduncanlivingston.com **page 214:** Mark Lohman, architect: Burdge & Associates **page 215:** Joseph DeLeo **page 216:** davidduncanlivingston.com **page 217:** Eric Roth, design: Dahlia Kitchen Design **page 218:** davidduncanlivingston.com **page 219:** Tria Giovan

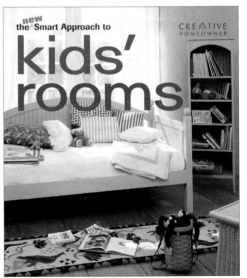